My Life After The Dwarves

More Sex, Drugs, Debauchery & The Devil

By

Vadge Moore

Babiazna ✶ Publishing

My Life After The Dwarves
More Sex, Drugs, Debauchery & The Devil
2023 © Vadge Moore
ISBN: 979-8-218-25594-7

Introduction
Danny Bland

Dedication:

This book is dedicated to all those who saved me from myself: J., Danny Bland, Blag Dahlia, Caren W., Stanley Wilson, Thelma Gatlin-Wilson, Gregory Thompson and everyone that worked at New Perceptions Alcohol & Drug Treatment Center. Without their help I wouldn't be alive today.

INTRODUCTION
BY
Danny Bland

WE aRE not Saints.

Of all the thoughtfully compiled wisdom, the selfless bounty of hard-learned lessons and the otherworldly yet simple caring direction the Big Book of Alcoholics Anonymous has to offer us (who so desperately sought it) it is those four words that changed my life. We, they said, even me, trying to hide my shaking hands in the pockets of my treatment center issued pajamas, was part of this; this gang, this family, this secret society, whatever aesthetically pleasing term I could swallow for the next 24 hours. We were lowlifes, criminal degenerates and miscreants with something divine to offer. I was accepted in that society for the exact same reasons I was rejected in every other aspect of my life. That simple sentence conveyed the message that we weren't and never would be perfect and that it just didn't fucking matter as long as we were there. Not only were we there to help ourselves but maybe, just maybe, we could (gulp) help others too; as in do something unselfish for the first time in a very long time if ever.

Vadge Moore is not a Saint. In fact, not since David Carr's "The Night of the Gun" have I read something so raw and relentless that I had to take a break between paragraphs, close my eyes, breathe deeply and whisper "would you please get it together, motherfucker" before continuing. I panicked for a character that I knew survived because I was reading Vadge's own goddamn words about these horrific events right there on the page. It is a testimonial to the miracle of the resilience of the human body that he could endure such a self-inflicted beating.

This is more of a confession than a memoir and although Moore is not seeking forgiveness, we the readers absolve him of his past indiscretions because we too, are not Saints.

Contents

Drink to Death

I'd start off in the morning guzzling at least three beers that I left on my bed-stand the night before. I opened the beers before going to sleep giving me quick and easy access to the poison-juice just as I woke up. This was how I kept the anxiety, terror and morning shakes away; kill that evil fucking sobriety before it had a chance to jump on me. Ok! Three beers almost done, now off to the bathroom. There I would shit, piss and maybe puke; I held my third beer in my hand as I sat letting everything go; flushing the toilet I'd make my way into the kitchen where a big bottle of red wine waited for me. I'd dump the vino into a dirty glass, raise a shaking hand to my mouth and gulp the medicine down.

All fucking right! We are feeling a little better now. Opening the fridge I'd reach in for my first cold beer, cracking it open I'd slurp half the can in two chugs; feeling a little less shitty it was now time to survey the rest of the apartment. I looked carefully around the flat because I never knew what or who I might find: broken glass, a passed out body, a dead body (!?); I just never knew what surprises might be waiting for me. This morning all I saw were empty beer and booze bottles, books tossed around, the TV on and a big, red vomit stain on the throw rug. Dammit! I knew better then to mix red wine with vodka and Jack Daniels; it happens every time! I opened the laundry room door and grabbed some towels to throw over the top of this disgusting mess.

This is me less than a decade after leaving The Dwarves. I'd been married (to J. from the previous book), my Mother had died (she lived to a ripe-old age of Eighty One) leaving me, my older brother and sister her condo in Mill Valley, Ca to sell; I'd taken my share of the money and bought a one-bedroom condo-flat in Midtown Atlanta, Ga and as you can see, I'm slowly drinking myself to death. J. has left me to my own devices as she's taken a job in Ft. Worth, Texas. My leaving the drug and alcohol-fueled punk band The Dwarves has not curbed my appetites in the least! If anything it's only gotten worse; without the discipline of rehearsing, recording and touring with the band, things that kept my drinking kind of in check, I now was free to drink a massive amount of booze with no distractions whatsoever. To make matters worse, on the first floor of our building there was a bar-restaurant; no surprise I was spending a lot of time down there. I guess, knowing that I lived in the building, the bar manager F. put up with a lot of bad behavior from me, including hitting on some of the female employees and, one night, vomiting all over the bar-counter. After "unloading" and collapsing on the floor, F. picked me up, put me back on my stool and told his bartender to give me another drink. "You'll be fine, my friend." He told me. "When you fall off a horse, you get back on and ride again, yes?" "You're right, F." I slurred "Another glass of wine and a shot of Whiskey! I'll feel much better!"

If I recall correctly, F. was Armenian and I suspected he was connected to mobsters from that country; he seemed to like me for whatever reason, but I always got the feeling that he could have killed me at the drop of a hat if he wanted to. There was a short time when we had prostitutes hanging out on the street corner. They didn't annoy me, I was used to that kind of company, but F. didn't tolerate any of that shit; one night he stormed out of the bar, dragged one of the prostitutes into the back parking lot and gave her what sounded like a beating. There were no hookers in our neighborhood after that! Too bad; I missed them. I never paid for their services, I wasn't into that particular vice, but every so often when I was drunk and alone I could find one of them to keep me company and give good conversation. They didn't seem to mind. Funny enough, I did enjoy some male hooker company for a time. I'll get to that later.

Atlanta was an alcoholic heaven; not only was there a full bar and restaurant on the bottom floor of my building, there was another bar on a street a block away from Peach Tree where my building was, there was also The Vortex bar and restaurant a few blocks down and a bar restaurant name Gordon Biersch a block away, another bar on the opposite side of Peach Tree that had a Gay night every week, and in the other direction near the Fox Theater there was another bar and restaurant! A liquor store was across from The Fox and a Publix Supermarket with a bunch of cheap deals on beer and wine a few blocks away down from Georgia Tech University. To top it all off a strip club was right next to The Publix! It felt like the entire city of Atlanta was trying to kill me; but I'd have a hell of a good time getting to my grave.

I loved to sit at the big windows in my flat looking down at Peach Tree and 5th streets and drink and drink and drink watching the people go by. Just a few blocks down past The Fox there was Emory Hospital; this is significant because just a couple of years before I had been admitted to that hospital for deep pains in my lower back. I tried to drink the pain away but it just kept getting worse; J. finally convinced me to check into the emergency room at Emory. "Fuck!" I thought to myself "I've finally done it; I drank my kidneys into failure! That's it! I'm dead! I'll have to live on dialysis or die a painful death while all my organs shut down!"

Once at Emory the doctors gave me the once-over, the twice-over and the thrice-over and finally came back with the diagnosis; my pancreas was about to explode. My what!? What the hell is a pancreas? I found out that the pancreas converts food into fuel; when booze is guzzled by the drunk it turns into stuff that is toxic to the pancreas. So, I was right! I was drinking myself to death. The strangest news was hearing from my doctors that my liver and kidneys were in great shape; my pancreas had taken one for the team!

I spent seven days at Emory hooked up to machines and a tube running from my dick to a colostomy bag; I had to wheel the bag into the bathroom whenever I had to shit, which wasn't often since all I was allowed to eat was jello. When I finally checked out my doctor told me that if I had one more drink I would die. After getting home from the hospital I think I kept my sobriety for maybe seven weeks; I kept drinking and I didn't die.

In fact, here I was, two years later; J. is in Ft. Worth and I'm inhaling more booze then you can shake a stick at. I was also getting deeper and deeper into the writings of Aleister Crowley and Kenneth Grant. I needed to take this interest to another level; I didn't want to just read about Magick and Thelema (Thelema is Greek for Will and is the name of Crowley's Magical system) I wanted to experience it. I took this time in Atlanta to begin Thelemic rituals as described in Crowley's books; I used the high-ceiling and wide open space of my Atlanta living-room and began two rituals: The Star Ruby, which clears away outside forces and The Mark of The Beast which pulls the Thelemic powers in; these powers are code-named "The 93 Current" for technical reasons I won't get into here. With these rituals I was getting ready for my "salvation"! Yep. It was not Jesus and his angels that would lead me off the road of self-destruction; it turned out to be Satan and his Legions! I'm half joking here, but Thelema does end up saving my life. But first I had to suffer through a shit-ton of ordeals brought down on myself by my own weakness and addictions. I still had a lot of sex, drugs and rock n roll to get through before I could be saved and this is the story of that terrible path.

MURDER MONKEYS

I was working on a tree crew permanently after leaving The Dwarves; no more touring or merchandise money to keep me afloat. I was a ground man that carried brush and logs up and down hills and dumped them into the truck; I'd use a chainsaw to cut the brush so it could all fit into the back of the truck and I got on tall-ass ladders to help trim the trees. And I was fucking drunk the whole time. Before getting home at night I'd usually buy a pint or two of vodka and pour it into a half empty bottle of water which I'd leave in the bushes by my apartment. I didn't want J. to know how much or how often I was drinking. Each morning I'd have to pull the snails off the bottle that had attached themselves' over-night. Not quite as glamorous as snorting lines of coke off stripper's tits and drinking free booze at the club.

I'd occasionally work a side-job with a tree crew guy named P. and he loved drinking on the job as much as I did; in fact he loved to purchase some coke or meth each morning and smoke and snort it up beforehand. Frequently we'd just bag the job and stay at his apartment getting high as fuck. Sometimes he'd lose his temper on the job and toss his chainsaw to the ground in my direction! It's a good thing that coke and meth kept me alert or I could have been pretty heavily injured.

J. had gone to the doctor for a check up to find that she had developed an ectopic pregnancy; this is when an egg attaches itself to the uterus and it can easily lead to the death of the woman. Even though I'd been pulling-out every time we fucked, somehow one of my tenacious little sperms had been able to complete its' mission. She called me from the hospital saying that she had to go in immediately for emergency surgery and that she could die. I scrambled out of the apartment and got to the bus stop, but not before I stopped at my favorite liquor store for some booze. When I was let in to see her at the hospital after surgery she could smell it on my breath. "What did you expect?" I yelled "This whole situation is very stressful for me!" Stressful for me; this is the perfect example of the egocentric narcissism of your typical alcoholic.

Meanwhile I was still in the bands Phoenix Thunderstone and Neither-Neither World and periodically doing some recording and occasional appearances with my experimental band Chthonic Force. Neither-Neither World arranged some shows in Japan, which was great because I'd never made it out to the Far East with The Dwarves; it was bizarre being in a country so different from the western world where hardly anybody spoke English; but the one language we had in common was alcohol. Japanese love to drink and we were staying in Tokyo at the home of an artist named Ru'; he made sure I had access to booze day in and day out! We drove out to Kyoto for some shows and on a day off were told we could go on a hike in the hills to a Buddhist Monastery or Temple; I thought I should lay off the drinking until after the hike and thank god I did. The papers recently had alerted the people that killer monkeys had been snatching babies out of cars and scampering off with them! On our way up the hill our tour guide informed us of this but told us not to worry; chances were good they'd just watch us at a safe distance and leave us alone. "I'll beat a monkey to death if it gets near me," I told my companions; which sounds great until you actually see a large group of them staring down at you from the top of a hill. In my shaky, hung-over state I timidly reached to the ground for a big stick to defend myself; a lot of good that would do me! "Fuck," I thought to myself "I'm gonna die in the hills of Kyoto eaten by some rabid fucking monkeys!"

As our guide had promised the monkeys kept a safe distance all the way to the Buddhist Temple. The Temple was gorgeous and the Monk there treated us with kindness and respect. We had to remove our boots, but once inside the atmosphere of peace and serenity was overwhelming; the exact opposite of my normal state of mind. The temple, the shrines, the foliage around the place that was maintained daily with minute care was pretty stunning to see. We were served tea and given a quick history lesson on the Temple interpreted through our guide.

As the day progressed I got more and more shaky; I was detoxing and needed some booze pretty damn quick. We still needed to complete the long hike back to the car, but this time I hardly noticed the killer monkey's; I was too wrapped up in my panicky need for some more liquid fire. I don't recall the return trip that well but I was able to purchase some Japanese beer before we got in the car; once back to Tokyo my heavy drinking resumed.

Punks, Drunks & Cokeheads

J. and I were getting pretty serious so I knew it was time to take the next step; marriage. She'd always told me that all anyone had to do was purchase a plastic ring out of a gumball machine and she'd say yes. We were coming out of a grocery store when I saw it, the machine. I told her we'd need more wine and asked if she could go back inside and get some; I'd wait here with the groceries. As she hurried off I turned to the machine. There were rings but there were also a lot of furry, unidentifiable children's toys; I didn't have long. I popped in a quarter, turned the handle and...children's toy! Dammit. Try again; quarter, handle...toy! Fuck! "Come on Satan," I said "give me that ring. I've served you well over the years so do me one more favor!" Quarter, handle and...ring! It was so cheap you could see the painted-on plastic was chipping away, but it would do.

On our way to the car I handed her the ring and said, "Oh, by the way...will you marry me?" Ah romance. Her face broke open in a big grin and she said, "You remembered, you actually remembered! Yes, of course I'll marry you!" And so began the first step in the next dozen or more years of my life. You could almost hear the gates of Hell open beneath me. It wasn't really that bad, we had some great times together but my constant drinking always got in the way. And yes, I did buy her a beautiful wedding ring later.

The wedding took place in Denver where her parents lived and it was also a good middle ground for my family and members of her family on the East Coast. My Mother and my Sister were there; also Blag and Hewhocannotbenamed from The Dwarves plus all of Phoenix Thunderstone because We had arranged some shows for us in town days before the wedding, which wasn't so bad because it helped me shake off the wedding jitters. We also had a separate wedding ceremony put on by the Occult Order I was a member of with Boyd Rice; I've described this ceremony in the previous book; it was a bizarre affair with a ritual I had written based on the groups Neo-Gnostic Satanic doctrines. Boyd Rice was the High Priest and attendees had to wear hoods over their heads as they were lead down into a basement; there they were treated to a ritual that espoused our beliefs in the balance of Creative Force/Destructive Force, Dark/Light, Christ/Satan, Hate/Love; over-all it was great ceremony and everybody had a blast. Later that night we held a concert starring the recording artist Ralph Gean; booze was imbibed, cocaine was snorted and the party went on into the early morning hours.

The next day it was Justice of the Peace time! The real legally-binding ceremony was a tame affair in comparison. That didn't stop me from drinking whisky from a flask and snorting blow off the toilet seat in the Court House bathroom. The reception was held at the Oxford Hotel and not a stranger collection of diverse people could you find anywhere: there was my Mother, my Sister, some cousins, J.'s family including uncles, cousins, her Mom and Dad, her Step-Dad and then there were the drugged-up fucking lunatics that were our friends: Blag and Hewho from The Dwarves, members of Phoenix Thunderstone, Thomas Thorn from the Satanic-Techno band Electric Hellfire Club and various acquaintances. Satanists, Sadists, Masochists, drunks, junkies and coke fiends; I'm sure the Oxford security was on high alert that evening.

We spent our honeymoon in New Orleans; a week at a beautiful hotel in the French Quarter right across the street from a 24-7 bar, in typical New Orleans style. The door was never closed. We had a big balcony and we'd sit out there every evening drinking wine and getting a good buzz going for the nights festivities which generally included moseying on down to a seedier local bar which catered to our kind of people: punks, drunks and coke-heads.

We went on a touristy Ghost-Walk whose host showed a group of us around the Quarter where much murder and mayhem had taken place; he'd describe the unholy events and regale us with stories of spirit-hauntings and the like. We could tell that this guy was one of us; so I approached him afterwards to inquire where we could obtain some blow and where the late-night parties were happening. He loaded us up with cocaine and whisked us off to a private bar where we spent the remainder of the blurry evening snorting, drinking and dancing.

It went on like this for the rest of the week; we had a blast. There was only one problem; even with our beautiful Hotel, the romantic setting, the sexy-spooky atmosphere of New Orleans, I had no interest in consummating our marriage. It didn't even occur to me; I just wanted to get loaded and stagger around New Orleans with my new bride. J. mentioned this toward the end of our stay and I immediately made it right; however, this was a sure sign that something was wrong. I, the great womanizer, Dark Lord, sex-driven maniac had to be reminded to fuck my wife on our honeymoon. This was a warning sign that all was not well and would only get worse.

R.I.P

More things occurred in the next couple of years that gave me a great excuse for heavy drinking; the 911 attacks in New York City and more personally my sister calling from my mother's house saying that she found Mom unresponsive on the floor of her bedroom. It seems Mom had a massive stroke and was on her way to the hospital. More booze! After J. and I loaded her trunk up on vodka, wine and beer we tore off to the hospital. Me my brother and my sister stood around the bed watching this machine pump air into her lungs; the only thing keeping her alive. I was just worried that somebody would smell the booze on my breath, but nobody said anything. It had to be a mutual decision with me and my siblings on whether or not we could pull the plug on Mom but when the Doctor asked for an answer my brother and sister looked to me. Mom always told me that if she were ever in a situation like this that she wanted to be let go; and that was my answer. Another great reason to drink; somewhere in my tortured brain I thought that I could blame myself for her death and take my drinking to another level; so I did.

After the nurse pulled out the air tube she stayed until Mom's breathing ceased completely; when her pulse stopped the nurse laid Mom's hand on the bed and left the room. The three of us stood by the bed in silence; I think my sister was weeping a bit and I recall my brother staring at the bed, a pair of dark sunglasses covering his eyes. I knew he was upset because I never saw him wearing shades indoors. I stood there stunned.

I guess at some point my Sister and Brother had left the

room but I didn't notice. I approached the bed. I stared at my Mother's corpse; I whispered gravely, my voice cracking a bit, "You know, you weren't really the greatest Mother. You probably didn't discipline me enough, but you always let me go my own way. You might not have been the best parent, but you were a great friend. I love you, Mom" I reached out, touched her arm and walked out the door.

DEVIL WENT DOWN TO GEORGIA

Me and the other siblings sold Mom's condo and split the cash. J. had completed her Master's Degree in Art History and we were free to get the fuck out of Dodge. I'd been chomping at the bit to get out of California; too many memories, ex- girlfriends and burned bridges. It was time to move on. The goal was to eventually move to Atlanta, Ga; that's where the High Museum of Modern Art was and J.'s dream was to get a job there. Her Aunt offered to let us stay for free in the basement of a home she had in Charlottesville, Virginia. Her Aunt was a devote Jehovah's witness so any shirts or statues that extolled Satan or Thelema would have to be kept out of sight, especially my Dwarves shirt embossed with the lyric "Teach Children to Worship Satan!"

J. did land that Job at the High so it was off to Georgia. First we rented an apartment on Myrtle and Ponce De Leon streets; our next door neighbor was an attractive gay man who seemed to have a never-ending stream of young guys in and out of his place. "Holy shit, I thought "I'm living next door to the homosexual Vadge Moore; awesome!" Using my inheritance money we purchased a flat in Midtown Atlanta. As mentioned, the area was an alcoholic Nirvana, booze galore! Having been there touring with the band I knew I'd love Atlanta. J. told me that since I had invested most of my money on the flat that I was free to stay at home and work on my writings. I had a book inside me waiting to get out and this would give me the time to work on it. I've always loved the American South; the heat, the people, especially the women; the South was my kinda town! I seem to remember catching scabies from a young lady I had sex with while on tour but that certainly didn't change my feelings for Atlanta. I couldn't believe I was going to own my own home. I'd only rented shitty apartments in bad parts of town my whole life, so this was a new experience for me.

When we were in Charlottesville my drinking had slowed down considerably, but when we finally landed in Atlanta my drinking revved up to enormous proportions. Not working a day job I stayed at home and worked on the book; I also began drinking form the moment I woke up to the minute I went to sleep. Since J. was at work the whole day I could imbibe without worry or guilt; she'd usually be home after five and as we all know, only a drunk drinks before five. Once she got home I'd be half in the bag, but I could hide it pretty well. My whole life people had told me how great I was at holding my alcohol; while everybody is dropping like flies, I'd just maintain a steady drinking pace with hardly any bad effects. If they only knew what I was experiencing on my end!

I was getting deeper and deeper into Crowley's Thelemic Magickal system and would perform masturbatory sex rituals every day, along with The Star Ruby and Mark of the Beast rituals. Years later I'd discover that this Magick actually works; I was calling forces to myself that would significantly change my life forever. At the time I just thought it was great that I could cum all I wanted, perform Magick and follow in the footsteps of my hero Crowley. I'd stumbled across a website called Aiwass.com which is run by a man who would end up becoming my Thelemic mentor, Nemo Pandragon (not his real name). I'd also been delving into the Voudon Gnostic system of Michael Bertiaux, which is a very powerful occult engine based on intense sexual energy. I was in heaven!

I've had some pretty astounding experiences through Magick and they can't all be attributed to my enormous drinking problem. Those experiences increased a thousand-fold after I had sobered up and they continue to this day. We'll get to that later.

BOOKS OF PERVERSION & BUCKETS OF BOOZE

Here I am; J. is at work and I'm drinking and staring at a blank page. I had to write this book! I knew it would be based on the Greek word Chthonic; which I had discovered while reading Carl Jung. This word called to me and when I looked deep into its' meaning I understood why: psychologically it represents the dark subconscious impulses of lust, hatred, perversion, violence and murder; of course I was drawn to it! I'd named my band after it, Chthonic Force, and I'd been swimming in those impulses for many years through my obsession with the work of the Marquis De Sade. I wanted the book to be a literary expression of those impulses but I also wanted it to explain in linear form what chthonic means and who has expressed it through their art and philosophy over the years. I needed prose and theory. Once I finished the theory part I then needed the prose.

In order to find some modern day inspiration I began reading all the books of a friend of mine, Peter Sotos. His books are a kick in the gut; they're usually written from the vantage-point of a predatory, sadistic pervert so I knew they'd be just the juice to help me cook-up a batch of sickness. Sotos' works are much more insightful then what I just described but they'd be a great inspiration for my purposes. I also knew that alcohol would be a great inspiration, so I'd start drinking early and begin poring over Sotos' books with a heaping helping of De Sade to boot. Later in the afternoon I'd jump in the elevator and ride down to the first-floor bar. At some point I made the acquaintance of a nice young man who lived a few doors down from us; he had a raging thirst for booze and cocaine too so me, he and J. would frequently purchase a few eight-balls and hoover very long lines off of our living room counter.

About this time Blag invited me and J. to come see The Dwarves in Baltimore, party and maybe sing a song or two with the band. Hell yeah! It gave me a chance to see the boys, visit with some old friends and drink and snort to my hearts' content. It's all a drunken coked-up blur but we had a great time. We were eating and drinking at a local establishment when I looked up and saw the legendary film maker John Waters! He's made some of the greatest movies ever including Pink Flamingos, Multiple Maniacs, Female Trouble and Hairspray, to name only a few. I saw him stare warily at me as I drunkenly approached his table. "Mr. Waters, I'm sorry to bother you but I just wanted to tell you how much you've inspired me and my band. We're The Dwarves and we're playing just down the street. We'd be honored if you'd attend." I don't remember quite how he responded but he politely brushed me off and thanked me for the compliment. Needless to say he didn't attend the show but years later he'd be the host of a punk festival where he announced The Dwarves before they hit the stage.

Once we were back in Atlanta it was business as usual; books of perversion and buckets of booze. This is when my pancreas decided it had had enough. Seven days at Emory Hospital and then I yanked the tubes out of my arms and decided it was time to go home. Even with the Doctor's warning of my eminent death if I even had one more drink, I kept drinking. I did stay sober for about seven weeks after the Hospital and was able to finish my book: Chthonic Prose & Theory. It's not a bad book, it might even be a great book; it's had a handful of fans over the years but it never sold very well. At the time I didn't care; I just had to get all that shit out of my brain and onto the page.

J. didn't know that I continued drinking and I don't have a clue as to how I kept it a secret, but I did. She'd be sleeping and I'd sneak out of bed and pull the bottles out of their hiding places and start guzzling. I'd be asleep before she woke up and relatively sober by the time she got home. Every time she went to go visit family or friends out of town, I'd stay home and drank like a fish. Sneaky drinking is very stressful but also a lot of fun! I definitely experienced a rush from concealing this, lying and slinking around. I could still be a bad boy even if I wasn't on tour with the band. It allowed me to commit slow suicide.

J., under the false impression that I was sober now thought that a quick vacation to New York City would do us some good. She wanted to fly to NYC, stay at a beautiful Hotel over-looking Central Park and take in the sights; go to the Museum of Modern Art, the MET and visit an old friend of hers that owned a bar in town. Problem was how was I going to maintain my drinking with her always by my side? It was a puzzler. I came up with the idea that honesty, or almost honesty would be the best policy; I told her that I had been experimenting with a beer or two while she was at work and I found that I could stop when I wanted and that it was no longer a problem. She bought it hook, line and sinker! If I kept my drinking down to only a beer or two at a time, this would be acceptable; I knew I wouldn't actually do this but I would figure out the details once my drunken boots were on the ground. Off we flew to NYC.

Drinking was kept to a minimum, I didn't have to sneak around; we'd go out for lunch or dinner and I'd have a beer and then stop. You'd think I might have realized this and maintained my equilibrium once I got home, but no. When we visited J.'s friends bar I acted perfectly normal. But I kept myself situated at the bar-counter where I could order extra drinks when J. wasn't looking. After catching a little buzz J. and I got hungry for blow and of course that was easy to obtain. We tracked some down, trotted into the bathroom and began keying blow out of the baggy. Ah...just like the good old days!

Once we got back to Atlanta all bets were off and my drinking went right back to my extraordinary standards. J.'s mother and father in law moved to Georgia, forty minutes outside of Athens and every time we visited I could indulge the booze-fiend. Her father in law drank a lot and I had ready access there all the time. Everything seemed fine to me, but of course there'd be a wrench thrown in the works that would up-end everything.

My Own Private Alamo

We're settled in a home, I don't have to work, can drink and write and practice my rituals. What could possibly go wrong? What went wrong was that J. was sick of her job and tired of her boss. After a quick search she found a museum in San Antonio, Texas that would hire her, we scouted the area for a home to put money on which turned out to be only a few blocks from the museum and we settled in; again. We rented out our Atlanta home so we had some extra cash coming in, but I was becoming increasingly unhinged. I don't know if I would have gone completely off the rails the way I did if we had remained in Atlanta but fact of the matter was I felt that I'd been dragged across the country and still didn't feel like I had a solid base-camp.

On top of this, as if to welcome me to San Antonio or maybe as a foretaste of the typhoon my life was soon to become, one morning while J. was at work I look out the window to see a violent storm brewing that just kept getting worse and worse. At one point the trees in our backyard are literally being blown sideways. Holy shit! What the fuck is this!? After the storm has died down I head to the store to pick up my booze for the day and on the main street that ran parallel to our house I see cars and debris tossed everywhere; I see a couple of SUV's on their sides and another that had been almost completely torn in half. Some local onlookers tell me that a tornado about twenty to thirty feet tall had come roaring down the street picking up and throwing aside everything in its path! Fuck me! All of this within a scant 20-30 seconds; welcome to San Antonio Vadge Moore. Now you're going to die!

I was chomping at the bit to get away from all of this and the perfect opportunity presented itself; there was going to be an

Esoteric Book Conference in Seattle Washington and David Beth, the head of the Voudon Gnostic organization that I was a member of was going to give a lecture. To top it off the following week Voudon Gnostic founder Michael Bertiaux would be having a book launch in his home town of Chicago. It was decided that I would attend both events.

For months I had been courting various women online; yes, I had started reverting back to my old Vadgey ways. I had been trolling for some willing female participants and had found quite a few that were more than happy to engage in "sexting" with me; for those of you that don't know that's texting with benefits. I began amassing a rather large collection of naked female masturbatory pictures in only a few weeks' time. One in particular had caught my eye; she was a redhead with beautiful pale-white skin. She was also an exotic dancer of the burlesque variety so this really piqued my interest. I had decided to use this book conference event as a means to get my drunken claws into some new female flesh. This dancer lived in SF so it would be an easy trip for her to fly from there to Seattle; as for the Chicago book launch I arranged for a "friend" to fly from her hometown to Chi-town and stay with me there. This was a devastatingly beautiful woman that I had somehow convinced to cavort with me online; she lived in the Midwest so she would have a fairly easy flight from her home to Chicago.

I had convinced J. that this double-trip would be a good way for me to expand my occult writing career and give me a good ego outlet that I had been sorely missing ever since leaving The Dwarves. J. arranged my flights, my hotels in Seattle and Chicago and made sure that I had plenty of money on the credit card so I wouldn't go hungry or, god forbid, thirsty. She still believed that my drinking was being maintained at a reasonable level; it was not. Off I flew to Seattle!

When the dancer and I first saw each other in the flesh it was like waves of lust just rolled off of us. I had spent the last decade trying to contain the impulses, sexual or otherwise that life with the band had allowed me to indulge in; now it all exploded out me. We checked into the hotel, devoured each other in the elevator and burst through the hotel room door, dying to rip off our clothes. We staggered to the bed, pulled back the sheets and...BED BUGS! I kid you not; the middle of the mattress was a festering sink-hole of bed bugs. I've never before or since seen such a collection of these little vermin. This was a very nice hotel; you would not think for a minute that a place of this caliber would be infested with such things, but there they fucking were. The combination of all the booze I'd been drinking on top of the frustrated, violent lust that was searing through me hit me like a ton of bricks.

I stomped down to the elevator, fuming; I exploded into the hotel lobby yelling, swearing and kicking over several potted plants on my way to the desk. I was livid and causing quite a scene. I threatened to kill everybody in the building or some such ridiculous bullshit if they didn't fix this problem immediately; the book conference had brought people from all over the world so there were no more rooms available. Much to the hotel staffs' credit they arranged for me and the dancer to get a free room at a hotel down the street. It all worked out perfectly because David's room was literally a few doors down from ours, we had a great view of the Space Needle and the room was more sleazy than the other one, but sans bed bugs. Just the way I liked it.

As we were settling in to our new digs the local police arrived at our door. I guess my homicidal outburst had convinced somebody to call the Law. I apologized profusely, explained the situation and that I was a little drunk after my long flight from Texas. Once they left I turned to my dancer, lust dripping from my skin; that's when I got an inspiration, something I hadn't done since my years with The Dwarves...I reached for my belt. Our sex had an intense element of the sadomasochistic and during our time together me reaching for my belt always got us both excited. We spent hours beating, whipping, spanking and biting each other; her pale flesh looked magnificent with welt marks and teeth marks all over her body.

My back became a scratching post with additional bites and bruises all over me. I didn't care if later the wife saw all of this, mostly because about the time I was landing in Seattle she had found a few emails between me and the dancer arranging this trip together. I explained that she wasn't able to make it and it was just me and David hanging out; I guess she chose to believe it. She was furious but not very surprised.

What did she expect; she had married Vadge Moore, the legendary coke-snorting drunk who went through women like tissue paper. Nothing could get in the way of my insatiable appetites. These are the things that I was telling myself, even though I had no band, one book out that was hardly selling and a massive drinking problem. The truth was that I was dying inside; I missed the attention of being in The Dwarves and I was determined to live that life all over again. I had never confronted the death of my mother or the vast collection of insecurities and neurosis that had been building in me my entire life. This was only the beginning of my troubles; I was on a sinking ship and playing the role of a defiant drunken pirate on the end of the mast while the boat beneath me was being engulfed by the waves; yelling, screaming, laughing, crying and waving my bottle of rum angrily at the sky. An attractive metaphor but what it really means is that I was trying to die.

Voudon Gnosis

The first day in Seattle the dancer went off to visit some friends while I had a meeting with the other members of the Voudon group. I was a drunken mess. I can barely remember what happened but apparently I made quite a scene, hitting on the female members of the group and one in particular that had a beautiful pair of breasts; I was pawing at her and making lewd comments. I was truly terrible. How somebody didn't punch me in the jaw I don't know. To this day it still makes me cringe to think about it.

Touring with a band that was widely known for this kind of behavior was one thing; in that context it's more like putting on a show for the fans. But without the band, in a completely different setting with people that couldn't give a damn about some stupid reputation or expectation, it was just dumb, insulting, ugly and pathetic. The time and the place to live up to that reputation was over; it was long gone. Somebody needed to tell me that because clearly I was unaware. Luckily, somebody did: the owner of Fulgur Publications. He had released a book of writings of the Voudon Gnostic group I was a member of La Societe Voudon Gnostique and was about to launch Bertiaux's new book and I had hoped he would release my books as well. After my stupid performance I knew that was never going to happen. He really let me have it, letting me know in no-uncertain-terms how disgusted he was with me.

The following day I stood up in front of everybody that had been present for my drunken shit-show and apologized, especially to the woman that I had mauled. I was definitely at a breaking point; I remember later that night ordering a strong drink at a bar and when the bartender took my money I suddenly broke down in a fit of uncontrollable sobbing right there. I wanted to fall to the floor, curl up into a

ball and die. Instead I downed my drink in one gulp and staggered out of the bar. Something in my head broke and for the
remainder of the trip I was very polite and well-behaved. The
book conference was great and David Beth's lecture was excel-
lent.

The dancer flew back to SF and I had a great night drinking
with David. The next day we were going to fly out to Chicago for
Bertiaux's book launch; I was very excited. Not just to meet Bertiaux, whose writings had an enormous impact on me, but I really
couldn't wait to get my hands on the woman I had been courting
online for months. We'll call her A. We were staying at a big hotel
which I discovered was literally a couple of blocks away from
Bertiaux's high-rise apartment. After a few drinks at the bar A.
and I scrambled to the elevator and our room. We spent hours
exploring each other. Sex with A. was not violent like it had been
with the dancer; sex was slow, deliberate and tender. I don't
know if my experiences over the last day or so had tamed me or
if I read something into A.'s body-language but I knew this was
not a woman I wanted to vent my sadomasochistic tendencies
on. I wanted to savor every moment with her.

The next morning we were back at the hotel bar. David
came down to greet us and told me that Bertiaux would be meeting him in the adjoining restaurant soon. Holy shit! Bertiaux is
coming here now! I can't wait to meet him. I was told that I could
introduce myself but that afterward he and David needed to be
alone to go over some business. Years ago I had spoken to Bertiaux over the phone; The Dwarves were in Chi-town and I got the
bright idea to look him up in the phone book and found he was
listed. I invited him to come to our show but he sent a represen-
tative instead.

Now here I was ten years later, back in Chicago and sure
enough walking up to the lobby door comes Bertiaux; heavy-set
with grey beard, using a cane and walking with a noticeable
limp. I couldn't control myself; I yelped, "There he is!" I went running over to him almost knocking the poor man down in the process. I told him what an honor it was to meet him, how he had

been such a huge influence on me over the years and that I couldn't wait for his book launch. He was very polite although a bit shaken up by my abrupt introduction. I shook his hand gently and watched him saunter over to David's table.

Wow. I had just met and almost injured Michael Bertiaux, the man who, along with Crowley and Kenneth Grant had been an enormous inspiration to me. This week was going to be great! Other people that I met during this trip were Michael Staley, Kenneth Grant's right-hand (or left-hand path) man, his wife Caroline Wise and Ariock Van de Voorde. All three I have kept in contact with and have seen again over the years and Ariock himself was a great inspiration for me when I decided it was time to get my shit together.

Bertiaux's launch was spectacular; it was held at a local occult bookstore, he signed copies of his books and gave a lecture. While he spoke it was as if I went into a trance; one could attribute this to the massive amount of alcohol I had been drinking but I know there was something more going on. Bertiaux had been in "communication" with many of the same entities that Crowley had and these same entities I myself would have experiences with years later. You could compare this to a tuning fork that resonates to a particular vibration; I was clearly resonating to whatever vibration Bertiaux was giving off. It was intense.

Meanwhile back in San Antonio the wife was moving rather quickly; she had discovered my emails with the dancer, although I had explained them away, denying everything. This she seemed to accept, however, J. had decided that she was not happy with her job there, decided to pack up and move back to Georgia leaving the beautiful house in Texas that I had already sunk twenty-thousand dollars into and rented a two-story home in Athens, Georgia, literally a block away from her sisters' house. I barely registered what was going on and continued my relentless, drunken activities; but I knew deep down that nothing in my life was secure; not my home, not my marriage and certainly not my increasingly unbalanced psyche. A. and I had one more night of tender, drunken sex and as I saw her off the following morning I started to cry. My whole life was crumbling around me and my only answer was to keep on drinking.

That day I got on a plane to Atlanta where J. would pick me up and take us to our new home in Athens. The crash was coming, I just didn't know when; I was going to hit rock bottom and the landing was not going to be gentle.

Nervous Breakdown

I land in Atlanta; I'd been drinking quite a bit before and during the flight. Now it was time to face the music. J. picked me up at the airport and as we were driving to our new home in Athens I expected anger, recriminations, accusations or maybe just stone-cold silence. I got none of these. She was happy, talkative, excited about her new job prospects and loved our temporary new home. As opposed to our single-story flat in Atlanta that we were currently renting out, this new place had two floors, two bathrooms, two bedrooms, a separate office room for me, a yard, a garage; holy shit! It was like we were living in the Beaver Cleaver household.

I thought to myself, ok I can settle in here; maybe I can even get a little sober. Yeah right! Not a chance. I kept up a jogging regime and agreed to only drink beer; but every chance I got I would head to the liquor store on my bicycle and load up on vodka to hide inside the house. I would try to stay away from the hard stuff when J. was around, but whenever she left town for a job interview I would hit the vodka hard. One time when J. was away her family came by unexpectedly to see how I was doing and found the front door wide open and me passed out on the living room floor. I have no recollection of this.

When she returned she found that I had practically destroyed the house and was screaming at her to get me a ticket immediately to San Francisco. I was acting like a trapped, rabid animal determined to escape. Why San Francisco? There was a documentary film premiering based on the life and work of my friend Boyd Rice; I had been interviewed for this film and fully expected that I would appear in it. More fuel for my ego and another chance for me to relive the fame of my Dwarves days. "I have to get to this premiere," I told her.

Also, the dancer lived in SF and was quite happy to have me stay with her. J., relieved to get rid of me, I'm sure, gave me some cash, money on the debit card and put me on a shuttle to the Atlanta airport. I refused to allow her to drive me, I insisted on going on my own probably because I had stashed some vodka in my bag and wanted to get good and hammered for my long flight to the west coast. I told J. that I would be staying with an old friend in SF and not to worry; I just needed to get a few things out of my system. Holy shit, was that an understatement.

When I arrived in SF the San Francisco Giants baseball team had apparently won the World Series at home; as I staggered out of the airport shuttle and onto Polk Street the entire city was going nuts, coinciding perfectly with my own personal nervous breakdown. The streets were packed with crazy, drunken Giant's fans. Awesome! I was crazy and drunk too! Reports later emerged of police being over-run by the huge crowds, broken store windows, cars and at least one bus on fire, a police car containing assault rifles was broken into and the guns stolen; there was video of a mob surrounding a car and pulling the passenger and driver out through the windows and beating them almost to death while the rest of the mob destroyed the car. There could not have been a better city to more perfectly mirror my own inner turmoil.

In the midst of this insanity I was ecstatically welcomed by the dancer; she whisked me up to her Polk Street apartment and we immediately began to tear our clothes off; we spent all night ravaging each other until the sun rose, when of course it was time for me to get more booze before the morning shakes started to set in. Thank Satan there were liquor stores on every corner in this town. I love SF! I spent the rest of the afternoon drinking and thoroughly enjoying the dancer's company; she made me feel right at home and being a Burlesque Dancer her energy was always geared towards sex, sex and more sex. I was in heaven.

Later, we made our way to the theater where the movie was set to premiere. The place was packed; Boyd Rice was a legendary SF anti-hero so fans came from far and wide to see this film. After tracking down the director and his girlfriend me and the dancer plopped right down beside them, ready for my appearance in the film. The director clearly noticed my ridiculous, advanced state of inebriation and quickly distanced himself from me moving his seat to the other side of the theater. I was making a thorough ass of myself; talking, yelling and hitting on every woman within my sight; even the dancer was getting angry. In my drunken state I used my cell phone to call Boyd so he could hear the crowd's reaction to the film.

I remember bits and pieces of the film but according to my date I did not appear in it at all. I was livid; there was no ego gratification at all in that regard but at least I had a gorgeous redhead on my arm and unlimited freedom as long as my money didn't run out. However, it appeared that the gorgeous redhead dancer was becoming increasingly disillusioned with me; I was clearly not what one would call a good date; drunk, obnoxious, flirting with everyone and everybody. Ten years away from touring with The Dwarves and I had completely forgotten the art of womanizing. I was simply a drunken, loud-mouthed clown. It's a good thing I still retained some semblance of survival instinct because I realized fairly quickly that I needed to switch gears, similar to what I had done at the Seattle Book Conference. After this night I was sweet as pie.

The dancer and her fellow Burlesquers were holding a few performances in Southern California and wouldn't I love to go? I sure as hell would! This escape from the prison of married life was looking better and better, except that I was still drinking like a fiend. Every once in a while it would cross my mind that only the previous year I had checked into the Emergency Room at Emory Hospital for almost drinking my pancreas to death; but I would quickly swat these worries away like a fly. "Fuck that!" I thought, "I'm the Satanic Superman and nothing can stop me!" I wasn't just living on the edge of death; I was barely clutching the edge with one fingernail. This did not slow me down.

UNiTED STaTE OF HORNY

Using my debit card we rented a car and took off south down the 101 toward Lala Land. Drunk and in a constant state of horny I couldn't believe this vixen was leading me to a show packed with Burlesque performers! I also had not been to Los Angeles since 1999 or 2000 so I was looking forward to frolicking again in this city of fallen angels. However, I knew I had to be on my best behavior; if I acted too out of control I could easily be kicked to the curb and left with no vehicle and nowhere to go.

There was a big show that we would be attending and the dancer would be performing. A legendary Burlesque Dancer would be the host. This was held at an outdoor amphitheater at the foot of the San Gabriel Mountains in Altadena, Ca. I had plenty to drink but kept myself relatively sober by running errands up and down the long steps of the theater for the performers. I had a lot of crazy anxious energy burning inside me so all this activity was for the best. All in all it was a great time since I kept my drunken werewolf in check, and the dancer and I got along wonderfully.

She had another smaller show in town that week so we basically hung out in LA and saw the sights. We walked on down to the Viper Room one afternoon and had a few drinks; we then headed on over to The Rainbow and low and behold there was my old buddy Lemmy from Motorhead. We had met once before in Chicago when The Dwarves had been set to play at the Expo of the Extreme festival. The Dwarves had cancelled but I still got to watch Lemmy hit on my future ex-wife. A decade later and I'm in much different circumstances, hanging with him at The Rainbow and downing a few Jack & Cokes. I listened to him complain about Blag; apparently Dwarves and Motorhead had played some shows together and it had not gone well.

That's The Dwarves for ya; we aim to displease. Lemmy also spent a fair amount of time hitting on the dancer. "Holy crap," I tell him "the last time we hung out you spent the night hitting on my wife, now you're hitting on my girlfriend. You're worse than me!" He chuckled/growled at me and turned back to his video game that he was notorious for always playing.

The dancer and I got some food, some more drinks and headed back over to The Viper Room; there was a show happening and the club was sold out. "No problem," I thought "this is where the name Vadge Moore comes in handy." And sure enough it did! The doorman was a Dwarves fan and happily gave us passes and drink tickets. Now my ego was burning on all cylinders; a redhead on my arm, my sense of self-importance inflated, free passes and drink tickets; it was as if I were back on tour all over again. But I wasn't, the money was going to run out and I had no plans on what to do beyond the next morning. If I actually had thought about my perilous situation I probably would have collapsed in a heap, but I didn't and I just kept chugging along.

We'd had a great week and I decided that instead of crashing on somebody's floor the dancer and I should get a motel room; and we did, right across the street from a gorgeous California beach. It was beautiful. On our drive back to SF we stopped at another beach, got out of the car and lay down in the sand. At one point I remember rolling on top of her to kiss her, looking deeply into her eyes, when something clicked. What the fuck am I doing? The exciting life I had been living the entire week came crashing down around me. I had left my home in Georgia, left my wife, I had flown out here on a drunken whim for a woman I barely knew and was drinking like a fish even though my doctor warned me it would kill me. Was I having a nervous breakdown, a mid-life crisis, what the hell was I doing? The dancer saw a change in my expression and asked me, "Darling, what's going on? Are you ok?" Sitting up in the sand, I laid my head on my knees then looked up and stared out at the Pacific Ocean, stared out as far as I could see. I quickly gathered myself and said, "I'm fine my dear, everything's ok; it's just been a crazy week. No worries."

But everything was not ok; I was starting to slip back into sanity. The repercussions and ramifications of what I had done were starting to dawn on me. I needed a plan, I needed a direction; something had to change. As we walked back to the car I had already made some decisions; I was going to have to leave the dancer. I needed to get some breathing space; then I needed to decide what to do about my home, my marriage, maybe even my drinking. The past week had been amazing but I was no longer in a band; every night couldn't be a Saturday night, this would not last. At one point we stopped to visit my old friend Ron Findlay; he and I had played together in our first band Crypt and later The Test Subjects. He had a nice home and had settled down with a lovely lady in San Luis Obispo. Why couldn't I be content with something like that? Why couldn't I settle down and be happy instead of constantly drinking and chasing after some fame that had slipped away a long time ago? Why couldn't I be with just one woman instead of running after anything with a pulse?

I had to figure some things out and once I got back to SF I needed to be alone and think; and also drink, of course. But I was starting to question that part of my life too.

Stumbling Down Memory Lane

I didn't know what to do; here I was stuck in SF and I'm starting to regret all of my decisions for the past month. I did the only thing that I could do, I called the wife; J. was surprisingly understanding. She got on the internet and found me a fairly cheap hotel in the Tenderloin District of San Francisco. I told the dancer that I needed some space and some time to think. However, I knew I couldn't just sit in this hotel room drinking and thinking; I needed to get out. After ten long years I was finally back in my hometown; I began to feel that I needed to look back over my life and try to discover where I went wrong and hope that I could make it right again. J. told me that I had a high limit on the card and that I should do whatever I needed to do to figure out my next step.

I called a taxi and drunkenly loaded myself into the back seat. "I want to go to Mill Valley, across the Golden Gate Bridge; I'll need you for a couple of hours. Can you do that?" Hell yeah, he could, and off we went. Seeing the Bay Bridge and the Golden Gate again was fantastic but there was a deep feeling of fear and sickness as well. As we drove through the heart of Mill Valley I took note of all the changes that had taken place within the last decade and also how so much had stayed the same. I told the driver to take me to the house of an old friend, a College buddy of my older brothers' knowing he would still be living in the same house. I appeared at his door out of nowhere, drunk and bleary eyed; he was not happy to see me; I was in pretty bad shape.

Feeling jilted from this encounter I then had the driver take me to the home where I was born. My Mother and I had moved out of this place when I was around four years of age but I retained a lot of deep memories from there. Once in front of it I felt that I had to see the inside. I drunkenly marched to the front door and knocked; it was answered by a nice couple who were a little surprised to see me. I explained that I had been born here and could they possibly allow me to look around inside; I was given a very polite no answer and I understood; a crazy, drunk stranger dressed all in black wanting to roam around in their home? Of course not; I told them thanks anyway and apologized for bothering them. In those few moments though I was able to peer inside and see the old hallway, a section of the living room and the stairs leading up to the bedrooms. It was enough to satisfy me. So many memories came flooding over me; as I left their porch I walked back to the taxi driver, paid him and proceeded to climb up the steep hill to a road I knew was at the top; a road that my Father had died on while riding his bicycle with his doctor. He'd died of a heart attack on that road when I was only five months old. I then followed this road on foot which took me back into the heart of Mill Valley.

I made my way to the Condo complex that my Mother and I had moved into after leaving the birth-home. It all looked pretty much the same except for the large park behind the condo which had acquired a bunch of nice, new plastic play-gear, climbing bars and slides. Plastic. When I was a kid we played on hard steel bars that had sharp edges that could seriously wound you! Kids today; wimps. This was also the scene as described in the previous book in which I had broken into my neighbor's homes for some late night fun.

I went to the court yard in front of the condo and stared at the front porch; old scenes played out in front of me: sneaking out of the house to see punk shows in the early eighties, running away from home to live in squats and vehicles hanging out with punks, drunks and junkies; I could see Blag coming to pick me up for a tour, Angel high on heroin swaying back and forth trying to conceal her nod from me, J. and I living here after I had moved her from Texas and I imagined the scene of the paramedics wheeling my dead Mother out the front door. I saw a lot of weirdness and pain; maybe I hadn't gone wrong, maybe it's been wrong all along.

I took a long pull from the water bottle filled with vodka that I had in my bag when suddenly I heard a voice behind me; "Tim, is that you?" I spun around to see the nice lady that had lived across the way from me and my Mom for years; holy shit, she's still here?! "Sally!" I yelled "You're still living across the way?" "Of course," she replied "What are you doing here?" She invited me into her home, sat me down, gave me some water, because she had no alcohol; and besides who drinks alcohol this early in the day? I sat in the chair and gave her the run-down of the last ten years, thinking everything was ok; but she started acting strangely, making excuses about why she had to leave, appointments she needed to keep, but the whole time I could see she was getting more and more nervous. She finally told me that I had to leave; that's when I realized how really drunk I was, how I had been rambling off this tale to her, crying a bit and acting pretty bizarre I'm sure. I said goodbye that it was good to see her again and staggered out of her door.

I knew it was time for me to get out of there and stop wandering around the streets of Mill Valley; the MVPD would not care if I was simply walking down memory lane; all they would see was a drunken middle-aged man wobbling down the street dressed all in black with tears in his eyes. My last visit was to the creek by the condo complex where I used to get high, play hooky from school and generally get into trouble; fittingly I passed out there. For how long I don't know; but when I woke up I was a little more sober and I was a tad more clear-headed. I took care of that problem by chugging a good portion of the vodka; I stood up and made my way to the bus stop. The Golden Gate Transit would drop me off only a few blocks from my Tenderloin hotel; the same bus that I had the sick, delirious ride after OD'ing on alcohol and Codeine.

While waiting at the bus stop I became filled with an overwhelming feeling of sadness and depression; what the fuck had I been doing for the last ten years of my life? Drinking constantly, wandering the country aimlessly; trying to plug up a hole in myself that seemed bottomless; what have I been doing? I knew I had to make some changes, I just didn't know what kind of changes or even how to begin making them. I was at a loss, sort of; deep down I knew what I had to do, I knew the first step I had to take, I just wasn't ready to take it yet. It would take a few more disastrous years to get there.

Operation Rehab

After spending some time at the Tenderloin hotel J. informed me that our card was running out of money. Little did I know that some things were being put into motion to get me some help; wheels were beginning to turn and I was completely unaware; nights I would stock up my room with beer, wine and whiskey and head out to the seedy Tenderloin streets to drink at bars in the neighborhood. The dancer kept texting me, asking how I was doing and when I would return to her; J. had been in communications with Dwarves' singer Blag to see if I could stay in my old room at The Dwarves house. He agreed to this and when I appeared at his door I was in pretty sorry shape. Blag conveyed this to J. and he and she started working on Vadge Moore: Operation Rehab.

Former Dwarves bassist Marky De Sade (aka Danny Bland) had spent time in rehab and had been clean and sober for years; in fact he left rehab in the '90's to join The Dwarves and had remained clean ever since: no mean feat! Blag had band business in Los Angeles to attend to but he gave me the keys to the house and sternly told me in no-uncertain-terms that I could stay there briefly but I was not to allow anybody else inside the house: nobody! I agreed.

I had stopped answering the dancer's texts and phone calls but imagine my surprise when one morning the bell buzzed loudly and I opened the door to find her outside in a terrible state of agitation. What was I doing, she asked? When was I going to come back to her? I couldn't just start this romance and then disappear, leaving her in the lurch! She was right; I had gotten her involved with my breakdown, my addictions and whatever crazy fucking mid-life crisis I was going through. I should never have put her in this situation and to this day I regret all the pain I caused her. But there was something else going on too; something that would make sense three or four years later.

She told me that a very large hawk had been flying around her apartment window; she said she had been receiving messages in dreams and trances to the effect that "They" wanted to contact me that "They" had something important for me to do. At the time I thought that she had completely snapped; I began to fear for my life thinking that this poor woman had become completely unhinged. But there was something to this: in Aleister Crowley's Thelema the hawk is very prominent, representing the Egyptian God Horus and Horus is the God that is presiding over this new era of humanity's development. This can all get very technical and occulty and this is not the place to dive deeper into what it all means, however even in the midst of my drunken stupor I recognized that this meant something; this was the first stirring of what was to become the absolutely strangest part of my story.

The dancer, so I thought, had ensconced herself on The Dwarves house front step. This made my ability to get out of the house and retrieve more booze Impossible. Was she really there? I didn't know; as I peered out of the front window in what might have been a paranoid delusion, I thought I had seen her but I wasn't sure what was reality or what was fantasy. For all I knew she wasn't there and I was letting my imagination run away with me. What I did know was that I was struggling with the beginning stages of alcohol DT's. I was in pretty frequent phone conversations with J. so I explained my dilemma; she told me to call the police and have the dancer removed from the premises, if she was even there. This I did. I also made a call to the red-head Texas girl in the previous book who we'll call K., who lived nearby to please come and bring me some booze. She was in touch with J. who was also in touch with Blag and Danny. K. was happy to bring me some booze after I explained my situation even though she had literally just been married and was now on her honeymoon. Later I realized this was all a part of Operation Rehab. When someone is in the advanced stages of alcoholism, cutting off their booze flow suddenly can lead to seizures, stroke and death and my shakes were getting pretty bad.

K. and her new husband were so kind and generous; they brought me a bottle of whiskey and sat with me for a time, talking about their wedding and other things; this quite possibly saved my life. They were both amazing; they didn't once show a hint of shock or disgust at my pathetic state; they were both simply kind, happy and very helpful. Meanwhile Danny Bland had put in a call to Music Cares, a charitable organization that, among other things helps musicians financially that desperately need drug and alcohol rehabilitation. I agreed to go to the southern California rehab center known as New Perceptions, located in Northridge. Man, I was really living out this stereo-type; forgotten musician addicted to booze and drugs fallen on hard times. If I could just survive so as not to complete the stereo-type of musician dead from alcohol and drugs!

It was tough getting in; the wait to get a room was a long one but thanks to Danny's help a room became available for me pretty quick. Between Blag's willingness to allow me to crash at his pad and Danny's machinations in arranging a room at rehab they both essentially saved my life which I will be forever grateful for. They along with K., J. and others, for good or ill saved me; you can aim your thanks or condemnations at them. J. couldn't get all the way to California to get me, Blag was out of town. My rehab room was available now; how the hell was I going to get to the airport in my scary condition? J. arranged for my cousin, who lived nearby to come get me and make sure that I made it on the plane. By the time she got to me I was an absolute mess. She later told J. that my room was a disaster, it smelled bad and that it was pretty damn clear that I was drinking myself to death.

Now I just needed to keep enough booze in me so as not to go into any type of seizure. I know it sounds counter-intuitive, but it's the truth: I needed to stay drunk so that I could survive long enough to get sober. I was given the phone number of a man who would meet me in LA at the airport. I spoke to him before boarding the plane in SF; "How will you know who I am when you come get me?" "I'll know who you are" he said in a rather dead-pan voice. "I guess you're looking pretty torn up right now; you'll stand out pretty good." Well, fuck. He was right about that.

I sat at the SF airport bar drinking as much as I could; wine, shots of whiskey, vodka and orange juice, whatever. I just had to make it to LA and these people would do the rest. What I didn't know at the time was that this would be the first of three trips to New Perceptions; the first two would not stick. Well, practice makes perfect they say.

New Perceptions

"Ok, give us your bag," she said to me "We've got to make sure you're not bringing in any pills, powders, plants or booze." This was Thelma and there was no doubt that she was in charge of this place. I was sitting drunkenly in the second story office of a two story building somewhere in Northridge, Ca. I don't really know what I expected, but it wasn't this; I thought this would be a hospital setting but this was more like a nice, hip version of the Brady Bunch house. I was still pretty loaded from all the booze at the airport and on the plane but I was being very cooperative because I didn't want to piss these people off and end up in some nasty gang-ridden Los Angeles jail.

My month long stay was actually pretty nice once I slept off all the booze; they kept me on Xanax the first week, one pill every four hours; I spent most of my time the first seven days nodding off to sleep on the living room couch while listening to all the drug and alcohol related stories of my house mates. There was a side-extension of the house where we had most of our meetings and shared our thoughts and feelings with the counselors. There was a huge backyard with a pool and a fruit tree which we'd pick from every day. My first thought once I'd sobered up was that I wanted to start jogging again and get my mind and body back into shape. The head counselor told me I'd have to wait a week so they could take my vitals and make sure I wasn't going to drop dead of a heart attack. Once the week passed I started a daily jogging-yoga regime in the back yard.

The stay at rehab was pretty fascinating especially since it was in the Los Angeles area and when the whole house would go out to the various AA/NA (Alcoholics Anonymous, Narcotics Anonymous) meetings around town I would almost always see some big-name stars in attendance. I'll mention one because he has been very public about his sobriety and recovery: we enter this church/elementary school; there is a long, thin room with the usual meeting chairs all lined up and the inevitable podium at the front. We all file in and sit down. One of the girls from my house begins lightly kicking me in the leg; I playfully kick back, thinking she's just bored and messing around. She keeps kicking me so I elbow her in the arm, getting a little annoyed with her now. She keeps kicking and elbowing me until I turn to her and growl, "What the hell is your problem?" She stares into my eyes, raises her eyebrows and nods to the seat on my left and elbows me again; I turn to my left and...there he is. Holy fuck, it's Hannibal Lector! Sir Anthony Hopkins is sitting right next to me at the meeting.

I'm not one to get star-struck; I've known and met a lot of stars mostly in the music industry, but in terms of film and Hollywood, not so much. Meeting Lemmy made me a little star-struck and if I ever came face to face with Iggy Pop I'd probably faint; but here was Sir Anthony Hopkins, next-level fame; he's won Academy Awards and been in some of the biggest Hollywood blockbusters of all time. He probably experiences this kind of reaction a lot and he probably noticed my house-mate kicking me; so he very politely turned to me and asked, "How are you doing today?" "Great, just great" I answered. That was it. This was no place to start pestering him about his movies and awards and asking stupid fan-boy questions; he's here to stay sober and so am I so I just leaned back and waited for the meeting to start.

Our head-counselor had encouraged me to share a bit of my story at this meeting as I hadn't done any sharing at the other one's; so I did: "My name is Tim and I'm an alcoholic..." and when I finished Sir Anthony Hopkins patted my knee and said "That was great, Tim; that was really great." Holy crap, Hannibal Lector just patted my knee! I'd heard stories about other stars from people at the meetings and I'll share one because both these guys have also been very public about their sobriety and recovery. One fellow told me that he was running security backstage at a big rock show, opened the door to a dressing room he thought was unoccupied and stumbled upon Ron Wood of the Rolling Stones and Ringo Starr of The Beatles hunkered down and surrounded by a haze of crack smoke! Might be true; who knows; but it definitely made me feel that if these two huge stars could fall into addiction and recover, so could I.

Even though this was the first of three trips to New Perceptions, what I learned at that house, at those meetings, with those counselors has stayed with me. I never would have gotten into the right head-space if it weren't for the people at New Perceptions. All that I learned there sank deep into my subconscious and has remained with me to this day; I learned from other's experiences and what I saw, heard and shared gave me the tools I needed to get sober. My sobriety is no longer a program that I have to follow, it is a deeply felt instinct and intuition that I carry with me at all times.

Along with Thelma there was another boss at New Perceptions; Stanley Wilson. He has recently passed away but the amount of good stuff that he has put into the world is beyond compare. Thelma might have been the stern warden but Stanley was the crazy uncle who could regale you with stories of his coked-up alcoholic adventures and then show you that even a crime-minded crack-head such as he could get sober. He told me a story about his wilder days when he was smoking a lot of rock; he and his friends decided they were going to rob a bank to pay for their drug habits, so they loaded up on crack and AK-47's. He said he burst through the bank doors, leaped up on the counter and started waving his gun around, screaming, "All you rich white motherfuckers gonna give me your money now or you're all gonna die!" I believe that's the incident that landed him in prison but also eventually set him on the path to sobriety. Between Thelma, Stanley and a great counselor named Gregory, New Perceptions ended up giving me the mental tools I would need to turn my life around. I thank you all.

I know some of you are thinking, "What about a Higher Power; did you give yourself up to God, to Jesus, to Buddha as you're supposed to do in the program?" Not exactly; my Mother was an atheist. She told me that she didn't believe in God but that she would never stop me from believing in whatever I thought was true. So what did I have? I had Thelema, the voluminous writings of Aleister Crowley, the rituals and practices that I found in his books and I followed this religiously, even at rehab. Every morning when I would go into the communal bathroom to shower, I would sit on the toilet, close my eyes and visualize the ritual chamber that I had created in my living room in Atlanta. Every day a few times a day I would visualize performing the rituals Star Ruby and Liber Reguli (Mark of The Beast), right there in the bathroom. During the afternoon I would read some of the Thelemic material that I had brought with me; The Book of Perfection as communicated to Aleister Crowley and James Beck, Beck's Riddle of Sebra and I would pore over the book The Portable Nietzsche translated by Walter Kaufmann, making a lot of penciled notes in the margins. This was my religion: Thelemic-Nietzscheism. I was making myself stronger and stronger every day. This proved itself to be accumulative; it took me a few years to get where I could firmly stand upright on my own two feet, literally and figuratively; but I was on my way goddammit, I was on my way.

DEaD WiLLY

My time at rehab was up. It was mandatory to write the person you had hurt the most a letter of apology; J. got her letter. She flew out to Los Angeles, picked me up and we flew back to Georgia; we were still at the house in Athens. I rode my bicycle to the AA meeting that was about a mile away; I went to the meeting every day...at first. After a while, instead, I would just bike around town. I found a path that led to the wilderness near a lake; this seemed more healthful to me than just sitting in a dusty old church listening to other peoples' stories of woe and self-destruction. After a time the old itch came back and I would bike to the liquor store, get a small bottle of vodka and cycle out to the wilderness path. It was a beautiful setting, perfect for catching a good buzz-on. I remember thinking, "I've got this; I don't need these stupid meetings and I can drink a little bit of booze and not go crazy. I'm fine, I'll be fine." Today I think to myself, "What an idiot!" But I know this was all a process that I had to go through and that I had not yet reached my "bottom" as they say in the program.

The lease was up for the people renting our Atlanta flat so we moved back in. As mentioned J. had taken a job in Ft. Worth Texas so for the time being she would live there and I would remain in Atlanta...alone. What could possibly go wrong? It was decided that my Mother-in-law would come check on me periodically to make sure I hadn't gone off the deep end again; there was an AA meeting literally down the street which I told J. I would attend every day. I went once; never went back again.

J. thought that maybe what I needed apart from writing was to get back into music again; I had so many talented musician friends and enough of a name for myself that surely I could find people to play with. We bought me a nice DW drum kit at the local Guitar

Center, found a rehearsal room and I began biking every day to the practice studio. This did slightly curb my drinking; it felt good to be back on the drums, smashing away like the old days. Hell, I'd been playing drums since I was barely ten years old; maybe this was what was missing. I started hatching a plan; I'd get back into good drum shape and then fly Dwarves bassist Nick Oliveri (aka Rex Everything) out to Atlanta to record with me. Where it would go after that I had no idea; I was just going to take it one step at a time.

Of course I was getting a little bored, lonely and horny. I was drawn to a very cute girl on Facebook who I knew was a Dwarves fan and started courting her. She began sending me very sexy naked photos so things really began heating up between us. Never one to only look and not touch we agreed to have her fly out to Atlanta and stay with me for a week. It was seven days of sex and drinking and she actually got me to visit places in Atlanta other than the rehearsal space, bars and the liquor store. However, something else was happening or not happening; this didn't calm my insane need for female flesh but it definitely made things a little uncomfortable. No matter what kind of sexy, kinky fun activity we engaged in, I could not get it up, the ole Willy was not able to stand at attention; this still didn't stop me. I had a mouth, a tongue and two hands; I could still satisfy a woman...I hoped.

The week was extremely enjoyable, I didn't embarrass myself, I didn't piss anybody off, when we went out on the town I didn't get drunk and scream or cry or break anything, but I never stopped drinking. From morning until night, it never stopped. At the end of the week we got her a cab heading to the airport; she was weeping and so was I but mostly I just wanted to get back upstairs to the flat and resume drinking.

Nick had agreed to fly out, rehearse and do some recording with me; I located a recording studio and an equipment rental place so I could get Nick the gear he would need. Rehearsals went well but playing with Nick and just rehearsing alone were two completely different animals. Nick was still in perfect recording and touring shape; he never stopped playing; he was and still is a rock n roll machine. The engineer that was going to record us was a brilliant young man named AJ; he had heard of The Dwarves, had definitely heard of Nick and he was pretty excited to work with us.

Recording started off nicely but within a couple of days there was a problem; Nick had, shall we say, some legal issues pending and he was not allowed to leave the state of California for the time being so he had to haul ass back to Cali. We had recorded a few tracks and one in particular called The Void made it to a seven-inch split single with HeWhocannotbenamed, guitarist for The Dwarves' solo project. Meanwhile I still had a weeks' worth of studio time paid for so AJ called a local friend, Pat Stone who was the lead singer/guitar player for a great Atlanta band called The Dirty Magazines. Pat came in and we started jamming together. Before the money ran out we recorded a number of tracks with just guitar and drums that were actually quite good. I planned on releasing it once we had finished as a Vadge Moore solo project called Vadge Moore's Slam Piece; this never happened. I still have the tracks and I might complete them and turn them into something one day.

The studio work was at an end but now I had some local friends to party with and of course I found something else to occupy my time: a girl. She was pretty damn spectacular and could actually match me in the drinking department. My alcohol induced pancreatic trip to the emergency room was only a couple of years behind me and I was not even close to slowing down.

ALCOHOL & ORGaSMS

The Dirty Magazine's favorite place to play and drink was The Star Bar in Little Five-Points Atlanta; Pat would drive to my house pick me up and off we'd go. One night we walk in through the back door and sitting at the bar was an adorable young lady that immediately caught my eye. She was slamming shot after shot so I knew I had found my next companion. Right off the bat she and I got along great; we started talking and flirting but I noticed that her friends were getting a little upset. When she went off to the bathroom one of her buddies told me that she was a lesbian and that I was barking up the wrong tree, but my band buddies were telling me that she seemed pretty interested and that I definitely had a chance with her. Of course I listened to my band friends.

After a ton more drinks she decided that she wanted to stay at my place, so we stumbled to her car and drove across town. We spent the entire night drinking and ravaging one another; I explained to her that my wiener was inoperable but that I could satisfy her in many other ways. Being a lesbian she told me that she had no problem with that; so began a torrid affair that would last on and off for months; she coming to my place for sex and booze and me going to her house for the same. Her friends were still very much against her relationship with me but neither of us cared; we were having too much fun. One day her friend let herself into my young ladies' house, opened the bedroom door and was greeted by the sight of me with my face buried between her friends' legs. She screamed, ran out the door and my lady had to throw on a robe and chase her down. I heard them talking and then later laughing. When I asked her what they were talking about she told me she was explaining to her friend that this was nothing serious, she was just having fun. That's what made our relationship so great, brief as it was. Later, however, I began having deeper feelings for her, feelings I never told her about; I concealed this because I was certain she would turn and run. For the time being we were alcoholic fuck-buddies and that's all each of us needed. We would sometimes go a week without seeing each other but when she felt like it she'd call me, bring a bunch of booze and stay at my place for a night of alcohol and orgasms.

My need for sex sensations didn't end there. The times I didn't see her I'd spend the mornings and afternoons drinking beer and wine and then head down to The Vortex bar and have some pints of PBR, shots of Jack and Lemon Shots. At this point I had regained a lot of the weight I had lost after joining The Dwarves. I was looking bad; my weight kept yo-yoing. After rehab I looked great; I had spent my time there really working on myself, psychologically and physically. Now I was mid-point between thin and booze-bloated and I'm certain no young lady I met at the bar wanted to go home with a drunken creep like me. I'm sure I looked like a pathetic loser hunched over the bar late at night, eyeing any potential sex-mates. To put it mildly, I had no takers.

So I did the next best thing; I began bringing homeless men up to my flat to spend time with me. I'd feed them, give them some booze and at some point the evening would degenerate into them sucking me off, which as previously noted, didn't have much of an effect; I couldn't come but it still felt great. Any kind of sex sensation was all I was after. For some I would get on my knees, put a condom on them and suck them off until they came; then I'd send them away never to be seen again. Why would I do this, you ask; with many years of excessive heterosexuality? I assume it came from a deep loneliness, a need for human contact and the ever-present obsession to constantly experience the orgasmic sensation and delirium over and over again. I'd spent my whole life chasing after that sensation and now I was getting it, literally, wherever I could.

It's not the fact that I was chasing this need with men that made it so disturbing; it's the fact that I was bringing homeless men up to my flat, endangering myself and the other people in the building. I didn't know who these fellows were, I didn't know their history: maybe prison, rape, thievery, murder? I didn't know and I didn't care; I just needed to experience delicious sex at any cost. This along with the booze was merely an escape from my life situation; I was not happy. Why? I had a wife, a home, money from my Mothers' estate, I didn't have to work a day job, was making music, writing books; what the hell was wrong with me?

As drunk as I was, I was still studying and practicing Aleister Crowley's Magick and Michael Bertiaux's Voudon Gnosis. Bertiaux wrote about a particular sex-magical method of homo-erotic, sadomasochistic lycanthropy that induces a primal-animalistic state of mind while in the throes of a violent delirium; right up my alley! One night I brought a young man up to my flat for just this type of sexual activity; of course he was not aware that we'd be engaging in lycanthropic sex-magic! At one point, in the middle of our "encounter" I began growling, holding him down on the floor and strangling him; he became very alarmed to say the least! He jumped up, threw on his clothes and ran out the door. I just sat in a chair in the living room, bottle of Jack Daniels in my lap and waited for the police to show up. They never did.

Sometimes in a drunken state I'd go into these fits; one day I picked up the bar stools in the living room and smashed them into little bits. Why? I don't recall; it didn't take much to send me into a violent tantrum. It could have been something as stupid as banging my elbow against a door frame, who the fuck knows. This was very reminiscent of the tantrums I would throw as a little boy, destroying my bedroom in a rage. We'll get to that part of my life in the final book of this trilogy.

One day my lesbian fuck-buddie picked me up and we drove off to her house for more drunken fun; I left the cats with plenty of food and water expecting to be back the following day. Apparently my Mother in Law, who had been coming to check on me periodically, had decided to come by with some groceries; when she walked in all she saw was broken furniture and empty booze bottles; the place looked like a tornado had hit it. She immediately gathered up the cats and took them to her home; when I returned the following evening the cats were gone. I frantically texted J. who informed me that her Mother got them both to safety and it was probably time for me to think about going back to rehab. Fuck! I thought; here we go again!

Sure enough, my rehab home-away-from-home reserved a bed for me and J. drove me to the airport; back to rehab. Second time is the charm? Hardly; everything always comes in threes. Something inside me knew that this second trip wasn't going to work but I had to do it; my life depended on it. How long would I be able to cheat death? Either my insides were going to explode or one of the rough-trade boys I kept pulling off the streets was going to kill me. I only had a few more chances to get it right. A cat has nine lives; I was running up to about sixty. Eventually the Grim Reaper was just going to throw up his hands and say, "Enough! Let's get this clown!"

Habits Die Hard

New Perceptions was starting to feel like a vacation home; it was like returning to summer camp; same old faces, the staff and counselors, and many new ones, the other rehabbers. When put into an environment where I couldn't drink at all it actually felt great; I got right back into my old routine of jogging and yoga in the back yard and reading a lot. As per usual there were the endless AA/NA meetings, constant group sessions, but it didn't feel like a task; I actually got some enjoyment out of it.

It was decided that after a month at the usual Northridge house I would follow that up with two weeks at a sober living facility where I would have more autonomy and the ability to come and go as I pleased. This place was nice with a huge kitchen and like the Northridge place, a pool. I was allowed to leave the house and go jogging in the neighborhood every day. Some part of me, however, saw these stints at rehab as just a means to give the liver, kidneys and pancreas a rest so I'd be in good shape to get back home and go on another sex-booze bender. Granted I wasn't outright admitting this to myself, but in hindsight I can see how these thoughts were bubbling away in my subconscious.

J. was in Fort Worth, Texas at a new job at this time and initially the plan had been to move in with her. I put the brakes on that idea very subtly and carefully. How could I possibly do any drinking and whoring around if I was trapped in an apartment with my wife? It wasn't gonna fly; I insisted that I go back to Atlanta and the Mid-town flat and although J. later told me she knew she shouldn't have let me go, she was just done with the whole marriage. I was too and had been for years. I wasn't smart enough to realize that without some kind of outside control I was simply going to spiral right down the drain.

In Atlanta I was back to my old habits; bars, girls, boys, early morning jaunts to the grocery and liquor stores and many hours of non-stop booze guzzling while I stupidly stared out the window watching the world scurry around beneath me. I was content in a strange, sickly kind of way; along with the emotional and psychological dulling that I was achieving with alcohol and sex I was also trying to dull the rest of my senses by keeping a constant barrage of loud music and television blaring at all hours of the day and night. I had a rotating CD carrousel that just kept going at all times and two DVD's that were always on the screen: Fear & Loathing in Las Vegas and The Dark Knight. I was trying to block out any messages from my subconscious that could alert me to my psychological and physical crisis, but most importantly I was trying to remain deaf to what Crowley referred to as my True Will. If you ignore your True Will then you will continue to breed tragedy and disaster in your life; I was trying to give birth to a monster; a tragic, stupid, deaf, dumb and blind monster.

The Atlanta girl and I restarted our relationship so when I wasn't picking men off the streets I was sleeping with her. J. would come out on the weekends and I would make a point to sober up somewhat when she was there. She usually stayed for only a day and a half so I could leave bottles of booze and cans of beer conveniently hidden around the flat. At night I'd wait for her to fall asleep and then I would sneak into my office and retrieve the booze. I would stare out the window for hours and get mildly toasted; as sunrise approached I'd crawl back into the bed and sleep it off. One trick I learned was to eat a handful of peanuts periodically to hide the booze smell. I guess it worked or maybe J. was just done giving a fuck; I couldn't blame her; I was pretty focused and dedicated to my constant inebriation. Nothing was going to get in the way of that.

J. moved in with her father in Denver and she had me out to his place for Christmas 2012. My drinking had to be seriously curtailed, but I made it work; I'd go on long jogs in the neighborhood and stop to pick up pints of vodka at the local liquor store. J.'s father also had a cabinet filled with bottles of holiday booze, the kind he only pulled out during Christmas when family was over. When no one was looking I put a serious dent in those bottles over the next few days. One day J. caught me; I had been hiding a pint of vodka under our mattress for quick and easy access. All I had to do was excuse myself from J. and her father, walk upstairs to the guest room, reach between the mattress and the box spring and guzzle away, followed by a handful of peanuts. I guess J. was curious and followed me up the stairs, catching me in mid-swig. She was pretty pissed off and I was pretty damn ashamed. You know those moments when you're caught dong something you shouldn't and the shame just washes over you like a fever? That's what I felt. It was horrible.

Later, in a much more healthy frame of mind I would realize that shame was something you felt when you weren't following your True Will; if you're on your correct course through life there is nothing that should make you feel that way, even if friends, family, neighbors, Church and State and the entirety of civilization condemn you; if you're following your Star, your True Self there is nothing that can make you feel ashamed; but I wasn't and I did.

For the New Year it was more of the same but worse; I don't know how it was possible but I was drinking even more than usual. One morning I woke up in the park outside my building, passed out on a bench. Man, talk about a vision of my future self that I definitely did not want to see. So, yep; you guessed it; it was back to rehab. "Three's a charm... if at first you don't succeed try again...the road of excess leads to the palace of wisdom." This last William Blake quote actually does apply pretty well to me and my experience; but it was still a long road to that palace and I wasn't quite done with my journey.

Angels Weep

At New Perceptions I immediately reverted back to the old routine; jogging, yoga and my internal Thelemic rituals. We did the usual group therapy sessions and tons of AA/NA meetings around the Los Angeles area. I stayed one month at the Northridge house and another at the Sober Living facility; again I felt great getting sober and learned a lot about myself during our sessions, specifically what triggers my drinking. The constant refrain that I will never forget is: you don't want to drink? Don't take that first sip, dummy! Easier said than done when you're an alcoholic.

A great experience during the Sober Living stay was when The Dwarves came to town and played a show near-by; I was given permission to attend as long as I brought one of the counselors with me. Blag greeted me with a huge hug (what other kind of hug is there from the big fella?) and then we retreated to the backstage area and reminisced about the old days and what the band was up to recently. He invited me to join them onstage to sing/scream a song or two; it may have been the first time I was ever onstage with The Dwarves completely sober.

After my time at Sober Living was up I flew back to Denver where J. was renting a little apartment. Things between us were dead; there wasn't any spark left, no romance and very little love; I was sick of her and she was supremely sick of me. I started seeing a therapist once a week but it really didn't seem to help; I was right back to my old sneaking-drinking ways. She was working at the Denver Art Museum so while she was away I'd jog and then towards the end of the day I would purchase a cheap bottle of white wine with the money I was supposed to be using for the AA meeting collection plate. We decided that maybe a California sobriety method would work for me, which meant I could smoke a little weed at night.

Somebody in Denver suggested I should do a reading of my book Chthonic Prose & Theory at a local book store called Mutiny Café; this might help me get back on track, move my writing career along and, who knows, perhaps open up further readings around the country. My old friend Lorin Partridge designed a flyer for the reading and posted them up around the city; Mutiny Café was great and very accommodating; they arranged my reading stage with a big high-backed, throne-like chair and a single lamp hovering over my shoulder; it looked very creepy, satanic and gothic. About an hour before the reading I told J. and friends that I had the jitters and needed to go for a walk around the neighborhood. "Please don't drink, Tim" J. pleaded with me. "Just walk off the jitters and come right back, ok?" "Of course" I replied "Drinking is the last thing on my mind; I just need to clear my head." I was true to my word; I didn't drink...for a good ten minutes because that's how long it took me to get to the liquor store down the street. I purchased a half pint of vodka and after guzzling that down I was ready to go! I washed out my mouth with one of those tiny Listerine bottles and headed back to the show; no one was the wiser. Hell, a half pint of vodka? Hardly enough to get my alcoholic brain rattled, but just enough to give me that good ole Dutch-Courage I needed to get onstage.

It wasn't a large turn-out by any stretch of the imagination, maybe twenty to twenty-five people but it felt good to be back in my old element onstage. The prose pieces I read from my book are definitely not for the squeamish or the moralistically inclined so some of the audience members who weren't aware of my past history ended up walking out in a huff; oh well, can't please everybody. Some Dwarves fans were there and I signed some old records, sold and signed copies of my book, packed up and headed back to the apartment with J. I could tell she was pleased with the reading and maybe even had a glimmer of hope that our marriage could be saved. We shared the bed together but I would usually stay up until late at night reading a book or getting on the internet. I'd usually have a small amount of booze stashed away somewhere and I'd sip on that and smoke a little weed.

Something started seeping out of my subconscious at this time. I started performing Thelemic rituals in the apartment living room while J. was at work. Things began to change, to alter inside and outside of me; I don't know how to describe it except that certain energies began to permeate the apartment and affect my mind in many strange ways. When I would go for a jog in the neighborhood my attention would be drawn to numbers on apartment buildings and license plates; they always had some connection to Thelema. Thelema is based on the correspondence between numbers, colors, gods, elements etc. that can be found in the Hebrew mystical system known as Qabalah; numbers associated with Thelema kept popping up: 333, 418, 13, 11, 93 and 78. Everywhere I went, especially on my jogs these numbers would present themselves to me. I know anyone not familiar with Magick will see this as text-book psychosis of some kind, but in Magick this is very common. On top of this, at night when I would smoke a little weed I would go into trances and have some very vivid visions. I felt that, through my rituals I had opened some kind of doorway and something was getting through.

One day something happened that would completely change my life. I was a big fan of the TV show Sons of Anarchy and I would periodically post something on my Facebook page and make comments about the show. Somebody named Tellulah Belle would "like" my comments each week or make a passing comment herself. At one point I had mentioned something about respecting the TV shows' characters for their almost Nietzsche-type nihilism but then I added, "However, I'm not really a nihilist myself; I have a particular set of beliefs." "What might those beliefs be?" Tellulah inquired. "I'm a Thelemite; I believe in Aleister Crowley's Thelema and have studied and practiced it for years." If you listened closely you could have heard the Earths' axis shift, Angels in Heaven start to weep and the hooves of mighty Satan himself begin to dance a jig. Things would never be the same for me again.

PLEASE ALLOW ME TO INTRODUCE MYSELF

Author's Note: The experiences that I describe in the following chapters will sound insane to many. Some will assume that I'm lying in order to spice up the narrative or trying to play-off my "Dark Lord" satanic image; many more will ascribe what I've experienced as delusion and fantasy brought on by my over-indulgence and addiction to drugs and alcohol. This is certainly understandable. These are not normal experiences; they transcend the ordinary and the everyday. However, there will be others that will recognize these strange encounters as being their own. Whatever your reaction, know this: I am simply describing what I experienced, and what I perceived as real. I'm not standing on a pulpit and trying to gather a flock in order to spread a particular message; all I'm doing in these books is trying to express clearly and honestly what I have lived and what I have seen. At a very early age I became fascinated with Magick and Aleister Crowley and I struggled mightily to try and understand his system and to live it; in this I succeeded. I have always felt that I'm being watched and protected by forces unseen by the eye yet as real as anything we can perceive through our normal senses. I described in the previous book that I intuited the presence of this protection; the experiences described in the upcoming chapters confirmed my suspicions. Try to read this with an open mind. Many have come before me that describe something similar; in the recent past the well-known and respected author Robert Anton Wilson wrote of his experiences in his book The Cosmic Trigger; I hope you can give me the same benefit of the doubt that history has given him. So we proceed...

After I described to Tellulah (a Facebook pseudonym) who we'll now refer to as KM, what Thelema was she later told me that after the

course of a month she began to have visions she didn't understand; she felt as if the ground gave way beneath her and the
whole world shifted. At her Grandmother-in-law's Baptist funeral
all Hell literally broke loose. She began experiencing intense
spontaneous orgasms without the need to even touch herself;
as she continued to describe this to me I realized she was show-
ing all the signs of a kundalini awakening. In Hinduism kundalini
is a form of divine feminine energy located at the base of the
spine; it's also known as The Serpent Power. This energy rises
up the initiates' spine awakening centers called chakras that are
located in different places along the spine. As the kundalini rises
it induces great feelings of love, bliss, deep awareness and the
ability to communicate with intelligences not of this world; it
also brings intense colorful visions. This was clearly happening
to KM.

At this time she was the owner of a bar in Alabama and had
many responsibilities during the day; suddenly she had to meet
those responsibilities while in the throes of deep, penetrating,
debilitating orgasms. This might sound like fun to others but to
KM it was continuous, mind altering and it severally interfered
with her day-to day business. She also began to see things in a
very non-ordinary way; for instance, one day at the store she
began going into a trance with orgasms and visions; the lights in
the store changed drastically, or so she thought, and she suddenly felt that she was no longer in her body; although she was
still experiencing the orgasms that come with the body; as she
looked at the people around her she was horrified to see that
their faces looked like rubber masks or putty; some looked
normal but then others looked like they were ageing and decay-
ing right before her eyes.

Other times she was having visions of being in a stone
room on an altar and performing sex-magic with multiple part-
ners; at the end of these rites all the participants would orally
consume the seminal and vaginal secretions as well as the menstrual blood. This is Thelemic sex-magic 101 which KM had
absolutely no knowledge of; she had never read any books on

Magic let alone any books by Crowley and she would certainly have a tough time finding descriptions of these rites as they were supposedly secret. These rites were described in detail by Thelemic author and student of Crowley, Kenneth Grant but his books were extremely hard to find (as opposed to today where all of them can be found on the internet) and even more difficult to understand. All of that said, being the owner and GM of various businesses most of her life she certainly never had the time to study any of this material as it takes years to fully comprehend; yet here she was describing esoteric rites and practices in a matter of days that most practitioners don't understand after a period of years.

She told me that in her visions (and she emphasized they were visions, not dreams) a Dark Man kept coming to her and would speak in a strange language that somehow she could understand; her mind became filled with visions of music being played, dancing, bodies writhing on altars in stone rooms, menstrual blood and all the while experiencing powerful orgasms. The Dark Man tells her, "Say my name." She replies, "You tell me." He says "You know it." He then becomes a serpent and slithers between her legs, enters her, penetrates her entire body, comes through the top of her head, turns back around and bites his own tail, making a circle. When describing this to me she said she was filled with ecstasy, burning from the inside with visions and more visions, experiencing perfect, complete pleasure. She tells me that the name ringing in her head over and over was Lucifer; she tells me she couldn't even think of or write the name without having powerful orgasms.

You might be thinking: Oh man, Vadge is hooking up with a crazy woman who is having psychotic visions of Lucifer; so what else is new? I had doubts in the beginning too, until it happened to me. Keep in mind that this is simply correspondence through texts, emails and Facebook messages; as I'm reading all of this I'm wondering, "How do I know this is real? I don't know this person, have never met her in the flesh; this could be some kind of prank played on me by a disgruntled

Dwarves fan, a husband or boyfriend whose lady I may have slept with." As I'm thinking this I'm sitting at my computer desk in my kitchen in Denver reading her messages when suddenly my whole body becomes shot-through with intense electricity that was also powerfully sexual; when I call this sensation sexual that is a severe understatement! This was completely beyond any orgasm or any drug-induced ecstasy I have ever experienced before; this was huge and over-powering. What I can say is that this sexual-electric shock brought me to my fucking knees and I mean this literally! I was brought to my knees and then fell onto my back, vibrating with the most intense, pleasurable energy I have ever known; and it would not stop, it just kept going. I began to worry that J. would come home from work, find me lying on my back on the floor, writhing in ecstasy and would call an ambulance.

I was finally able to struggle to my knees, crawl over to the computer and type to KM "Make it stop." And just like that the energy went away. I fell to the floor again, laying my forehead on the linoleum and tried to catch my breath. "Holy shit" I stuttered "What the fuck was that?!" That's when I looked up at the computer screen and saw that KM had written, "You felt that, did you? That's what I've been feeling every day, non-stop for the last week without any break at all." I couldn't even imagine what that must be like; how a person could stand up and walk let alone carry out the responsibilities of a business owner while in the throes of this intense energy; it was beyond my comprehension; on top of this there were all of the strange visions she was having. I had no visions but, holy shit I definitely felt that energy! A portion of it stayed with me for the remainder of the evening. Apparently KM had asked Lucifer to give me a quick shot of kundalini to help me understand what she was going through.

Lucifer, huh? I've described Crowley's system previously; the turning point in his life was in the year 1904 when a preternatural intelligence by the name of Aiwass contacted him and dictated through him the text known as The Book of the

Law; an occult manual that announces the start of a new age or Aeon that will last approximately two-thousand years and will completely alter the world as we know it. Crowley himself described Aiwass as "...the solar-phallic-hermetic Lucifer." This new Aeon, ushered in by Aiwass-Lucifer is called the Aeon of Horus and it emphasizes the mental, physical and spiritual freedom of every individual on the planet; for, as The Book of the Law says; "Every Man and every Woman is a star," meaning a self-centered, free-existent being who's only real option is to follow their own course through life, follow their True Will, or as another line from the Book says, "Do what thou wilt shall be the whole of the Law."

This preternatural being has many names and forms: in Egypt he was called Set, in Sumerian he was Oviz, Pan-Bacchus in ancient Greece and Rome, Shiva in India and Satan-Lucifer in Christianity, although this last example really came from the work of John Milton in Paradise Lost. He also has another name that was revealed to me and KM through trance-communications; it's the name of my publishing company: Babiazna. As an introduction to us he used Lucifer. Why not? Please allow me to introduce myself, indeed.

SEX STORM GOD

As time went on KM continued to have trances and visions; in many of them she was being initiated into various states of mind by the two Goddesses of the Thelemic pantheon: Nuit and Babalon as well as being continually visited by Aiwass-Lucifer. In one vision she was given a list of letters and told to send them to me; when she did I immediately knew what to do with them, more from a deep intuition than anything else: I took each letter and found its' corresponding Tarot Card in the Qabalistic Tables; each Tarot card was explained in great detail in Crowley's Book of Thoth; each card represented a message that Aiwass-Lucifer was conveying to me. After a little study I realized that each one of these cards had a common denominator and always a starring walk-on role by one Egyptian God in particular: Set. Set is known as the God of the desert, storms, disorder and violence. As opposed to simply being evil the God Set frequently has a role as helper and guardian; more importantly Set is an extremely sexual God that uses the "storm" of sex energy to initiate those he has chosen. Through the letters and corresponding cards Aiwass-Lucifer was formally introducing himself to me as one of his most ancient identities: Set.

On top of all this crazy shit happening KM and I were actually falling deeply in love; there was an intense bond and connection that seemed to transcend time and space; I know that sounds pretty fucking hokey but that's what it felt like. It was a love that felt extremely ancient; of course I still had a wife and KM had a common-law husband but we were both miserable in these relationships. We were beginning to recognize that we had a common destiny, something we shared on an intimate level, that there was something very important that we had to do together. KM was having further visions but this time it centered on a child; she was continuously shown a child that would be the human incarnation of Aiwass-Lucifer himself! Who was to have that child? I was so blind and stupid on top of frequently drunk that it didn't occur to me who was supposed to birth this being; I kept wondering, "How are we going to find this child, will he just appear, where will we look?" Eventually it dawned on my dim brain that the parents were going to be us.

I'm sure the reader is pretty credulous at this point: Vadge Moore let a woman trick him into thinking he was going to be the father of Lucifer's incarnation; what a maroon! All I can tell you is what I perceived and what subsequently happened. However, one should keep in mind that KM was a very successful business woman; she made approximately a million dollars a year through the bar that she owned, wore expensive clothes and jewelry, drove a nice car that she would replace every year, had a large home and a condo on the beach. If she were a woman out to gold dig what she thought was a rich punk rock star, she was barking up the wrong punker; she had just as much money and was just as secure financially as any punk star I ever met, if not more so; so you can cross that motivation off your list. She barely even knew of The Dwarves but does seem to recall seeing us back in the early '90's in Washington DC at the 9:30 Club; she'd never heard of us but her friends told her that she had to go see the spectacle that was The Dwarves. Many years later she remembered enjoying the show.

This was something else entirely; neither of us knew where this was heading but something much larger and more powerful was pushing us together and forward. Looking back I would liken it to a train rolling at very high speeds down the track, but even that doesn't do justice to the whole thing or the sense of extreme urgency we both felt. It was more like a Space Shuttle fired by high-powered rockets, jettisoning us both out of orbit and deep into space; this simple illustration also doesn't come near to describing the power and immensity of what we were both feeling at the time.

Meanwhile back on Earth, my drinking increases; I wasn't even hiding it from J. anymore. One night I head on down to the local bar and guzzle a bunch of dirty vodka martinis; when I return J. is livid; we get into a huge fight which I can barely remember. I want to emphasize that I have never hit, hurt or abused any woman except within the context of kinky consensual sex; even with all the trouble and conflict between me and the wife, I never hit her or hurt her in all the seventeen years or so that we were together. While writing this book I was in continuous contact with her because I wanted to make sure I got everything right and accurate; she told me herself that I never hit or hurt her; apparently this night was different. According to J. in the heat of our argument I came at her and threw her into the kitchen counter which knocked all the cabinets off the wall. I have no recollection of this; today I have immense loathing and guilt for allowing myself to reach that horribly low level. J. called the police so I scattered out of there as fast as I could; I still had my debit card on me so I stumbled on down the street to a local, very expensive Hotel and checked myself in; I spent a night or two there trying to figure out what to do. J. saw the charge to the card and told me she was going to shut the card off if I didn't move to a less expensive Motel; however the first two nights gave me the chance to wander the streets of Denver drinking and looking for parties and cocaine like some kind of feral animal. I recall a bar, a fella that obtained some cocaine for us both, a couple of hours hoovering the blow off the Hotel room table and some kind of party that lasted until the sun rose.

I didn't even think of alerting KM to what was happening; I'd never met her in person, we'd only been communicating for a couple of months, I was ashamed of the condition I was in and I really didn't think it concerned her. At some point I realized that KM was my only hope; J. was going to cut off my card and I would be left homeless on the streets of Denver, so I emailed her. When I recounted the events of the last forty-eight hours she immediately sent me eight-hundred dollars through Western

Union; I tracked down a cheap La Quinta Motel nearby and checked myself in; I was so happy and grateful. Never one to even contemplate suicide, that option had been rolling around in my brain; now I felt that a huge burden had been lifted.

DOOM OR DESTINY

Sure enough, the powers that be supplied me with a party partner almost as soon as I arrived at La Quinta; as I'm hauling my bags from the cab into my room I see him: fat, sloppy, drunk and very cheerful; also clearly gay. Here was David. I knew I was going to have to amuse myself for a time and here was amusement to the hundredth power! I don't remember why he was holed up in this dump; some problem with his mother I think; who was sick of his drinking. A thirty-plus year old man kicked out of his mother's house; that's a hoot; but was I any better? I was a forty-five year old man kicked out of my house by my wife who was sick of my drinking; equally pathetic. We'd be perfect party-partners. We immediately got along, but in the back of my mind I was a little disgusted by him; this would be perfect for my ego. I was at the lowest point in my life; homeless, drunk, pathetic and I needed someone to make me feel better about myself, someone to compare my sad state with and give me the confidence that at least I wasn't as bad off as this fellow. But I was; just in a different way.

He was a great guy and a fun, pleasant person to be around. He brought me some beer and pointed in the direction of the nearest liquor store; we made our way there where I loaded up on bad convenience store food, vodka, wine and beer. Whatever my future would be, how I was going to extricate myself from this sad state of affairs, I didn't know and I didn't care. I had what I needed; food, booze and a play-mate. We had a blast and the La Quinta was our fun-land at the beach, so to speak; at some point J. came over to drop off some supplies like razors, tooth brush, tooth paste, soap and other things. She peered through the door and saw David drunk and lying on the bed; J. cringed and I laughed; making her nauseous made me giddy.

It was a party that never seemed to end; at some point I recall a large, yellow stuffed duck that I had acquired from somewhere and I have hazy flashbacks of me naked running through the parking lot simulating butt-fucking this duck. Hunter Thompson in his book Fear & Loathing in Las Vegas describes periods of time that jump out at him as in a dream and you're not quite sure if it happened or you just imagined it happened; this was the case with me for a few days and nights. There were also some darker times as when David's friends came by with some meth and psychedelics; apparently these friends had some enemies' because I remember one night in which we all had to lie low in the room and stay away from the windows because they were afraid of a drive by shooting from some meth dealers that were owed money. I remember sitting on the floor of the room, leaning against the bed, drinking and giggling with David, but upon hearing a car slow-crawl past our room we had to be deathly quiet.

KM finally agreed to join me; she told me that she was going to need a few days to a week to get things in order but that she would drive out from Alabama; she was leaving her common-law husband, her business, her home, her expensive lifestyle to come and be with me in a cheap downtown Denver motel! Something very powerful was motivating us; something within me purposely ruined and brought an end to my seventeen year relationship with J.; something within KM was motivating her to give up her comfortable, expensive lifestyle. Aleister Crowley has written that when you truly enter the Thelemic path you must be able to give up everything at the drop of a hat, without considering the consequences. The Gods only give you one chance in a lifetime; if you don't grab the ring then you won't have another chance again; KM and I grabbed that ring. We were now hanging on for dear life.

KM had her escape plan worked out; she was going to wait for her husband to go to work and then gather as much stuff as she could fit in her SUV; she buys me a plane ticket to Houston, TX where she will meet me and then we'll drive back to Denver together and decide where to go from there. I'm getting a little nervous; I've never met her in the flesh, I've seen pictures she sent and we've texted and talked on the phone; we're both completely throwing our old lives away for a person neither one of us has even touched. The pictures she sent we're beautiful; she's a gorgeous blonde with pale skin and the most stunning blue eyes I have ever seen; the pictures she saw of me weren't very impressive. I'd been drinking for months since my final trip to rehab and I was slightly over-weight and bloated from the booze; this did not deter her.

When I landed in Houston I immediately made my way to the bar; she was running a little behind schedule which made me ecstatic! I could down a few more shots and a couple of pints of beer and maybe calm my nerves. I'd done a lot of crazy things in my life but this might be the craziest; my mind was in a daze and riddled with anxiety. I remember my boots clacking on the floor and the sound of my luggage wheels whirring behind me and I didn't know if I was heading for doom or destiny; maybe both!

She ended up being a few hours late so I joyfully began hitting local drinking establishments. By the time she finally arrived I was soused; when she walked into the bar I was speechless, flabbergasted; she was absolutely gorgeous! Her bright, blonde hair was like silk that flowed over her shoulders and back, her skin was translucent white and her eyes were an incredible penetrating blue. She literally glowed. I couldn't believe it. And to top it off, something that her pictures didn't reveal; she had an enormous pair of breasts; I mean enormous. Russ Meyer would have been beside himself. She paralyzed me with her eyes and said "Hi Tim." We finally meet. Until now I've neglected to mention her other quality that absolutely floored me; a deep, sexy southern drawl. And I mean drawl. I just stood there staring at her, unable to move. She's stunning, I thought to myself; and I look like...this; as I cast a glance at myself in the bar window reflection.

When I get nervous or unsure of myself I immediately resort to drinking; since I was already drunk the next best option was sexual stimulus, so I reached for her, drew her to me, sat her in the booth beside me and began rubbing my hand between her legs. I immediately sensed she was tensing up and uncomfortable and who could blame her?! A man she had never met in the flesh, who she had only spoken to over the phone and through social media correspondence was now busy trying to start a friction fire between her legs. I stopped and asked, "What's the matter?" She replied, "It's nothing, I'm just very shy." I was silent and staring at my feet. The over-confident lady killer Vadge Moore was gone; I now simply felt like a homeless, bloated, drunk loser that's probably going to be left to fend for myself on the streets of Houston because this beautiful woman couldn't possibly want to spend even another moment with someone like me; I was fucked. There was a deathly quiet as I tried to figure out what I was going to do when she left me, because she was definitely going to leave me.

"KM...you are absolutely beautiful; you're stunning. I'm just sitting here trying to decide what I'm going to do because now that you've seen my bloated, drunk, ugly ass you couldn't possibly want to stay with me." "What?!" She yelled "You are gorgeously handsome; you look fantastic! I didn't leave my life behind and drive all this way to just be with some loser. I love you." That's when it dawned on me that this relationship was definitely going to work; if she could look at this drunken mess and see no flaw we were definitely going to live happily ever after. Our preternatural chaperone had other plans though: we were going to live interestingly ever after, but certainly in love. We were both hungry and I needed a stiff drink; we decided to stop at a very nice Hotel in Houston for the night which also had a bar/restaurant. As we waited for our food I went to the bar to get us drinks; while there I decided to have a few quick shots of Jack Daniels while they made our other drinks; probably not the best idea. I brought our drinks to the table and saw our food had arrived; I dug in having not had a decent meal for a while. Living on convenience store sandwiches can have that effect on a person. I guess I was eating a little too fast or maybe those three quick shots of Jack caught up with me, but I suddenly leaped up from my chair and raced to the Men's Room where I hurled up the entire contents of my stomach, all over the floor and some into the toilet! When I returned to the table KM was completely un-phased; "Are you feeling better?" she asked. Oh man, I thought, I'm really testing her; what a great first date I am! We had the rest of our food wrapped up and headed to the room. The room was beautiful and KM still didn't seem in the least perturbed by my performance. As my final act, while we were fooling around on the bed, I felt it coming, ran to the bathroom and hurled again...all over the closed toilet seat! My god I was a pathetic loser! KM was still undeterred and got a cold cloth for my face; I laid my head on her lap and slowly dozed off. I was feeling a level of peace and contentment that I hadn't felt in I don't know how long.

Soul Mates

When we got to La Quinta we found a big bouquet of flowers; apparently David had the maid put them in our room. Very nice of him; however, after a quick introduction to KM he started to act a little weird. "I think he's jealous of me" she said. "What, of you? No, he's just a strange guy." But sure enough he was getting jealous and it showed itself at inopportune moments; KM and I started paying for another room right next door because, as she put it, the old room smelled like a brewery/garbage dump. Really? I hadn't noticed, seeing as I was still guzzling booze as if there were no tomorrow.

One day KM decided that she wanted to get her nails done and told me she'd be back in about an hour or so. David and I cracked open some beers, sat on the beds and switched on the TV. After an hour and a half I started getting nervous. "Where is she?" I wondered out loud. "Oh no, Vadge" David said "You don't think she's turned around and driven home do you?" "No," I replied "She wouldn't do that; not after all the trouble she's gone through. Plus, we're in love" "I don't know, Vadge. Seems she had a pretty cushy lifestyle that she's given up to be with you. Would you want to stick around in a motel with a couple of drunks like us if you were her?" He kept feeding my worry and my paranoia; I began texting her asking where she was. Another hour goes by and now I'm starting to panic. "Fuck!" I yell while draining another pint of vodka "She did leave me, didn't she? She went home! What the fuck am I going to do?" "Don't worry" David said cheerfully "You've got me; we'll get a place together and everything will be fine."

Fuck. Get a place with this slovenly piece of shit? I won't, I can't! Shit. She left me; I've got nothing, I've got no one. Dammit! What was I thinking, throwing everything away for someone I didn't even know?

In the middle of this complete melt-down is when she walked in the door; "Where the hell have you been?!" I yelled "I thought you left me, I thought you went home! I didn't know what I was going to do!" I then grabbed her by the collar and pushed her up against the wall, screaming in her face; "Why didn't you answer my texts, what took you so long?" This is when I first saw the face of a woman that has been strong, independent and willful her entire life; who has been the General Manager of a New Orleans bar and later the owner of a very rough biker bar in Alabama. She remained very calm and smiled right at me. "Sweetheart" she said "I will never leave you. The nail place took a little longer than I expected and I haven't been checking my texts because my husband keeps calling and writing me. I will never leave you, I promise." I slouched backwards, fell on the bed, buried my face in my hands and began to cry, sobbing uncontrollably.

"David" KM said "Will you please go back to your room; Tim and I need to spend some time alone together." "Ok" David said solemnly and scurried away like a wet rodent. She then held me in her arms; "I will never leave you, ever. We are soul mates, we are meant to be together. Our lives are just beginning and we have a lot to do." I held her close, looked deep into those fathomless blue eyes and whispered, "I love you; I love you so very much. Please stay in touch with me whenever you go away; I can't ever lose you. I don't know what I would do without you. Promise me." She kissed me gently on the head and said, "I promise." She's kept that promise, to this very day.

David was getting to be a pain in the ass and was clearly trying to sow discord between me and KM; so we located another, nicer motel a mile or two away. I looked back as we drove out of the parking lot to see David standing at the curb, tears in his eyes, waving sadly to us with the stuffed duck tucked under his arm; poor guy. I wonder whatever happened to him. He probably got his shit together and is now a wealthy doctor with a gorgeous husband and a two-car garage. Probably not, but I hope so. He helped me transition to my new life if only by being there when I needed a friend. Take care, buddy.

But First, Sex

Once we got situated in our new motel it was time to make a plan; but first...sex. We hadn't had sex at the other motel because David was always around but now we were all alone. We literally tore each other to pieces; we tore off one another's clothes, I ripped her expensive panties into two with my teeth, she scratched me and bit me and bashed me across the face a few times leaving scratches and bruises; I whipped her with my belt and buried my face between her legs for hours; we strangled and slapped each other; we both came, she over and over; we screamed, laughed, moaned and groaned all through the night. It was spectacular. Afterward we lay next to each other on the bed, panting uncontrollably, trying to catch our breath. "Well," she said "That was all-fucking right!" "Yes," I whispered "It fucking was."

When I woke up the next morning she was on her Kindle, "I'm looking at places for us to go" she said "and I'm looking at a beautiful cabin in Donnelly, Idaho. It's right by a huge lake and the whole town has a population of two-hundred and fifty people." Holy shit" I replied "You mean two-thousand five hundred people, right?" "Nope; two hundred five zero people." "Well that sounds fucking awesome! Let's do it!" So that was it; we packed up and started on our way; however, I was going to need some "supplies" first, namely booze. She was not keen on me drinking in her car but I told her I had to; if I started going through the DT's then we weren't going anywhere. We stopped at a store, got me a few half-pints of vodka; small enough to conceal one in my jacket and put the rest in the trunk for later. Stocked with my own personal bar we were now truly on our way.

It was over nine-hundred miles to Donnelly from Denver and would take us approximately fifteen hours; we decided to do it all in one-shot. Why not? I'd driven a hell of a lot longer while on tour with The Dwarves and KM had just driven half-way across the country, one fifteen hour trip was not going to deter us. Having never gotten a driver's license I wasn't driving anyway, just riding and drinking. One thing we hadn't counted on though; where we were going was the fucking wilderness; there were no shopping malls, no Pizza Huts and certainly not many gas stations; the largest city was Boise, Idaho and that was two hours from Donnelly. We didn't stop in Boise for gas because we figured we had many chances to get gasoline before we got to Donnelly. We were wrong.

You have to ascend a big mountain pass and once you got to the top it was a straight, though winding path down to the next little town; however, we were running out of gas and damn near on empty long before we got to the top. We started panicking; it was pitch black out, no street lights and we didn't want to have to pull over to the side of the road because we weren't sure if the side wouldn't just be a dangerous cliff-fall down into a canyon where our corpses would be eaten by wolves, bears, raccoons and deer! We just didn't know and didn't want to risk stopping the car because somehow it kept pumping little tiny tears of fuel into the engine and stopping and restarting it might use up that last bit of gas. So we just kept driving upwards and praying to Lucifer for help.

Sure enough, we got to the top, past the peak and started our descent; KM took her foot off the pedal and we coasted our sorry asses all the way into town. Problem was we were still forty miles from the cabin and once we got onto a level street we were going to need some gas. Another problem; this was a tiny fucking town and it was closed! I mean the whole town was closed, shut down, benches up, shades down, lights-off fucking closed. Gas stations had no one to take our money and that's all we had. KM had left her credit cards at home because she knew her husband could track down her location through them; my card had been cut off and was useless. She had a big sack-load of cash from her bar that she had taken from the safe, but that did us no good here. Amazingly she found three or four Gift Cards in the door of her SUV; I didn't think it would possibly work at a gas station pump but low-and-behold it did! We got twenty bucks worth of gas and we were back on our way.

It had been snowing so once we got to the cabin it was covered with a fresh sheet; we crunched our way up the porch stairs and looked under the mat for the key; nothing. I looked around the door frame; still nothing. I trudged out to the mail box at the end of the road; nothing. Holy shit; we made it all this way, almost fell off a cliff to be eaten by deer and now we were going to freeze to death right in front of our cabin. I prepared to break a window with a rock covered in a shirt when KM called the rental number, hoping it went to their cell phone and not an office; it was three in the morning, and as we saw everything was closed. She got through; KM apologized profusely for waking them up at this hour but explained we just got there and we could not find the key. "Oh" she told my darling "It's on the kitchen counter." KM paused... "Ok, but we're on the front porch, can't get inside and we're freezing." "Oh," the woman laughed "The door isn't locked, it's open! This is Donnelly; nobody locks their doors." Oh...my...God; I turned the door knob and the door swung wide open. KM and I looked at each other and just started laughing. "Fuck me" she said "We are idiots!" "Yes we are" I replied "But we're perfect for each other; perfectly stupid."

We turned on the lights, started up the heater, made some spaghetti with sauce that we found in the cabinet; I had a bottle of cheap red wine in the trunk with my booze collection which I opened. We both sat back on the couch, sipping our wine and holding hands. Just then there was a movement at the glass-screen door that leads to the porch; we saw a large fox peering in at us. We both looked at him silently for a minute and then he was on his way. Kenneth Grant had quoted Crowley in one of his books that sometimes Aiwass-Lucifer would appear in the shape of a fox; I think he was checking in on us to make sure we got there safely, because he certainly had some plans for us.

Blood Moon

Our first week at the cabin was very pleasant; it was the off-season so we had the whole area completely to ourselves. We ate, read books and watched DVD's because there was no cable; talk about roughing it in the great outdoors! We'd stroll down to the edge of the lake hold hands and drop our feet into the water; occasionally we'd drive to a near-by town called McCall and eat at what became our favorite Chinese restaurant, over-looking a portion of this large lake. It was perfect; well almost perfect. I was still drinking like a fiend and even trying to conceal the amount of my drinking from KM just as I had done with J.; when she'd go to the bathroom I'd retrieve some beers from the fridge and hide them under the guest bedroom mattress. Why? Because while I was trying to slow down my drinking I would start feeling a panic attack coming on so I would scramble to the guest room and quickly down a beer to put the brakes on the overwhelming anxiety. I thought this was better than having to explain to my new partner why I got panic attacks every time my blood alcohol level got low. I felt that if she knew what kind of a pathetic drunk I really was that she would leave me. Was I just going to repeat the same pattern that I had with my wife? I hoped not.

My raging alcoholism aside, the first week or two was incredibly blissful; KM even got to dive into my large collection of occult-magic books that I had brought with me from Denver. She started to recognize a lot of the same experiences that Crowley relates in his books, particularly in his book The Vision and the Voice; she began pointing to visions in the book that she had experienced too. On top of this KM and I were having amazing sex together night after night; I would ravish her body with my mouth, tongue, hands and cock; yes, my cock! It was working, praise Jesus almighty, it was working! She kept bringing me to the edge of an absolutely amazing orgasm and then pull-away until, after a while, along with my persistent begging she would finally release me into an orgasm that would vibrate my entire mind and body.

Every night we would read from a Crowley text called Liber Samekh and she would immediately get visions of Aiwass-Lucifer and other Gods/Goddesses from the Thelemic pantheon. She would see Aiwass approaching her with a very erect phallus and he'd begin penetrating her over and over making her experience ecstasy and visions unlike anything she had ever experienced before. We were having sex constantly, I was having no trouble maintaining an erection; when she was menstruating she would go into intense trances and our sex would be over-the-top incredible. This was when I saw, for the first time, what Thelemic menstrual rites were all about; I had read about them in Crowley's and in particular Kenneth Grant's books but I could never quite conceive what they really meant or the effect they can have on an initiate. I need to mention that a normal couple engaged in menstrual sex and orally consuming the semen and blood won't experience the same effect; but someone that has awakened the Kundalini or Serpent Power within their body will have very profound experiences. I was and still am not a "High Initiate" but KM definitely was and is; when she consumed the "elixir" as it's called, it sent her into fits and waves of ecstasy combined with visions, trances and dreams that put normal sex to shame.

It was clear to me from the way she was behaving that this elixir gave her a high beyond your common high. What is the purpose of all of these trances, visions and ecstasy? Crowley had always said that his Mystical and Magical system represented the "next step" for humanity; these experiences will create mutations that will advance the evolution of the human race. This mutation wasn't only spread through DNA and human offspring; it also and more importantly is spread by a current of energy; what Thelemites call the "93 Current". I could feel this current just by being around her; I got a taste of it in my kitchen in Denver; a year or so later I would see it effect people around KM in many ways, mostly people would tell her that they felt "dizzy" around her, people at her work would say that just being in her presence would affect them strangely. This wasn't just a fantasy invented by our minds; we could see the current's effect on people around her.

KM told me that Aiwass-Lucifer was very happy, that everything was going according to plan; we had fallen deeply in love, our sex was amazing and successful; but even with this all happening KM was very distraught and pushed beyond her limits of endurance. Some days I would hear her in the shower speaking to Him; apparently running water attracts Him and brings Him to her. One time she was yelling at Him and berating Him, telling Him that she didn't want to do this anymore and she just wanted to go home. He would tell her, as she descried to me later, that this was her True Will and that she must follow this through; it's her destiny and I was destined to do this with her. He would tell her that she was going through the Ordeal A, which was all four Ordeals combined into one; Thelemic Ordeals are psychological and physical challenges that are very intense that every advanced Thelemite must go through. I want to emphasize that this is not an unhinged woman; this is a woman who has maintained a constant and rigorous discipline through businesses she has run and a business she has owned. Even today she maintains this discipline; this is not a psychotic person; this is a very strong, realistic woman.

Some nights we would just sit on the sofa, watch DVD's and I would hold and stroke her soft, pale little feet, calming and relaxing her. She started getting visions and messages about a coming Blood Moon; that it was very important that we conceive our child during this eclipse. Going into town one day we looked at the front page of the newspaper and sure enough, a lunar eclipse was soon to occur and would create what is known as a Blood Moon. A precursor to it was occurring that night but the next night it would occur completely. Even though our sex was amazing and I was, for the first time in years able to maintain an erection, this added pressure of having to perform and conceive a child made me just a tad nervous. I got too drunk that first night and we didn't even attempt sex but the following day and night KM kept getting visions and messages; she was told to have me consult the Tarot cards and every time I did the message was that time was of the essence, we had a job to do, this was our destiny etc...

As the sun went down I started getting more and more nervous; I was drinking but not as much as usual. We began kissing on the bed and I could feel my cock getting harder; I suddenly grabbed her, tore open her jeans and mine, pulled my pants down to my boots, bent her forward over the bed and fucked the hell out of her until I finally shot my load of cum deep inside of her. That was it; she knew our child was conceived at that very moment. Aiwass had told her that it would be a boy and his name would be Jonathan Embry. At least we wouldn't have to struggle with deciding on his name; this was decided for us! I did a Qabalistic examination of this name and it described a monster of a Thelemic-Overman. Afterwards we kissed and stepped out onto our front porch, descended the stairs and looked up where we saw the Blood Moon slowly vibrating beautifully in the night sky.

Head in a Box

KM was certain that Jonathon was conceived that night of the Blood Moon so naturally she began to worry about money. My wife and I were filing for divorce and she was going to sell our Atlanta flat of which I should receive a healthy sum; I had put close to a hundred thousand dollars into it so I expected back at least that much. We didn't know when that money would arrive so KM decided that she needed to drive back to Alabama and regain control of the bar she had left behind. I'll never forget that day when she drove away; I knew we needed the money what with a child on the way, I knew she needed her very successful business back, but she was carrying our baby and I was extremely worried about her. I sensed that something was in the air and I didn't like it. I'd severely cut down on my drinking and had increased my daily jogging routine; but I also knew I'd revert back to heavy drinking once KM was gone. When she drove away I swear I had a vision or a glimpse of Aiwass very upset; he was furious. I could hear a voice in my head chanting, "No, no, no,no...." I would find out why soon enough.

Things did not go well on her return to Alabama; her husband is furious, angry and abusive. Aiwass had given KM a secret name to invoke whenever she was in trouble; this name would protect her. She completely forgot about this name and it's no wonder in light of the horrible details; she did not tell me about this until months later because she thought it would make me completely lose my mind and she was probably right. On her second day back her husband raped her; maybe once, maybe repeatedly; she isn't sure. She did her best to fend him off but he was simply too big and strong. When she finally got away from him she staggers outside to figure out what she's going to do. When she comes back inside the house he is in the lotus position on the floor, apparently in a trance; Aiwass has seized control of his body. He has a knife in his hand and is holding it to his cock, threatening to cut it off; KM told me later that Aiwass was trying to get her husband to kill himself for what he had done; KM in horror takes the knife from him as he comes out of the trance. This is not a man who has ever been in the lotus position before, never had anything to do with magic, mysticism or the occult; he's a "good" Christian, a military man but also a violent biker. Aiwass had clearly manipulated his mind.

In the middle of the night KM sneaks out of the house, gets in her car and speeds off driving as fast as she can; in her panic she drives off the road and wrecks her car somewhere in Montana or Wyoming. Since the car is in her husbands' name his phone is immediately alerted to the wreck. Later that day she is in the hospital when who should appear but her husband and his two nephews; his mechanic had a private plane and had quickly flown them to the hospital to take her home. The terror and the horror she must have felt I can only imagine. Once they got home the abuse only got worse. He tells her that he has tracked down the cabin where she and I were staying, possibly from following her SUV's GPS system; he had called rental places in the area and located her name and residence. In one of his abusive tantrums he threatens to cut off her head and mail it to me in a box. After hearing that our rental people were stupid enough to give out our location to a complete stranger, I smashed up a portion of the cabin; this time my violent tantrum may have been appropriate. I was in a rage, panicking and just wanted my sweet, beautiful darling safely back to me with our baby.

At one point he put a gun to her head; a few days later he calls his daughter from a previous relationship to tell her goodbye, that he was going to kill KM and himself. While he's on the phone she runs to her neighbors' house; finding nobody home she hides in the some bushes and calls her husbands' mother alerting her to what's happening. The mother says she's on her way and for KM to call the police immediately; the police arrive and arrest her husband. Now that he's safely behind bars she can make her escape; after she had wrecked her SUV he had bought her a tiny, two-door sports car that barely had enough room to fit two people let alone any luggage. She knew that he did this to insure she wouldn't be able to leave him again, at least not with any of her belongings. He underestimated her desire to be free of him. He laughed and told everyone that she couldn't leave him because nothing would fit in that car; she couldn't give up her designer purses, shoes or clothes not to mention the show-quality bulldog that he had also bought her. He said she couldn't leave him for fear that he would torture the dog, how without her bar and him she couldn't survive let alone make the eight-hundred dollar per month car payment. But he underestimated her desperation for freedom; he'd always thought of her as a little doll and never recognized or respected her achievements. That tiny car was her only means to freedom and nothing could have stopped her. Their relationship had always been cold and unfeeling; KM told me she never felt any love or affection from him; something she was clearly craving. His family, on the other hand gave her tons of love; since leaving she's deeply missed all of them and sometimes cries thinking about the time they spent together.

Back at the cabin I was a mess; the cabin also was a mess with beer and wine bottles covering the floor. I was trapped here with no means to travel except on foot; I'd walk the two and a half miles to the nearest liquor store and get more booze and food when I could; when I was too sick and weak to walk I would pay the one-man in town taxi service a large amount of money to bring me some on his own. I was incredibly relieved to hear that her husbands' in jail; she says she's got to put a few things in order and then she'll fly me out from Boise to Shreveport, Louisiana where we can make plans to settle down before the baby comes. Why Louisiana? She had spent a good portion of her life in New Orleans managing bars and restaurants; she thought that this would be a good place to relocate that was familiar to her. I didn't care where we went as long as I could have her back in my arms. I cleaned up the cabin as best I could, put all my books and belongings in boxes and bags; had my taxi guy take me on a two-hour drive to Boise where I stored my things in a U-Haul storage facility. I checked into a Motel and waited for her to call me about my flight out of there. Meanwhile there was a bar-restaurant in the building and a gas station convenience store right next door. No more hiking three to four miles to get my booze!

Things were bad; KM had been to hell and back, although I would not learn about all the horrible details until much later; my drinking was still out of control. We had no home and a baby on the way. On the plus side I would have money coming from the sale of my Atlanta flat, I was finally going to have the love of my life back in my arms and...we had a precious baby on the way. I remember thinking to myself, "Holy shit, this life I'm living sure takes a lot of crazy-ass turns." The craziness wasn't over; there were a few more bad turns along the way.

Good Place to Hang

All I had to do was get to the Boise airport, board the plane and sit in my seat for five hours; shouldn't be a problem. There was a problem. I had started drinking early at the Motel, I had booze stashed in my bag until I got to the airport; before going to the gate I scurried into the men's room and downed as many beers and as much wine as I could. Once I got my ticket and got to the gate I found a bar and started hitting the hard stuff; when it was time to board I was pretty lit. On my way to my seat I was sweating profusely and on the phone with KM; she told me a little about what had transpired between her and her husband, not the rape, but the gun and the abuse. I tried to keep my cool, not lose my temper but I could barely contain myself; I started cursing and swearing between gritted teeth as quietly as I could, or so I thought. Apparently one of the other passengers saw a man in a state of fury, sweating a lot and decided to alert the stewardess. Because of the terrorist attacks on 9/11 and incidents on planes since then there was a zero-tolerance policy towards anyone that looked a little disturbed; I clearly looked disturbed.

The stewardess politely asked me to gather my things and follow her; in my drunken state I assumed KM had somehow moved me to first-class; no such luck. I was escorted back to the gate and told that I had upset one of the passengers and they didn't feel safe with me on the plane. Can't say that I blame this person; I wouldn't have felt safe with me on the plane either! I was a mess. I calmly made my way to the waiting area, called KM and told her what happened; she immediately got me another flight…for the following morning. There were motels nearby but we thought it would be best for me to tough it out for a few hours and remain at the airport in case there was a change or an earlier flight. Of course I made my way to the bar and began drinking, but I drank slowly, no guzzling. I let myself get sleepy, set the alarm on my phone and slumped in a chair for a nap; I wasn't going to let my raging alcoholism screw this up; I needed to get to my love and our baby. I wasn't going to get so inebriated that I'd end up causing a scene that would get me arrested. I had to cool my fucking jets; so cool them I did and nodded off to sleep.

I made my flight without incident, land in Shreveport, Louisiana and make my way to the curbside terminal; KM pulls up in this very sleek two-door sports car, the one her husband bought for her. She has the top down and looks absolutely gorgeous; we drive to a cheap motel in Bossier City called The Mainstay that will be our home for the next couple of months. The contrast between this semi-trashy motel and KM's hot sports car was hilarious. The room has a little kitchen nook and a regular sized refrigerator with stove tops and an oven so we can save money on meals. We may have pulled up in a sports car but we were essentially homeless and poor; she had money that she retrieved from her bar and I would have the money from the sale of my Atlanta home. Unbeknownst to us at the time, from now on we would be living in poverty. I didn't care how we lived, as long as I could be with her.

She was definitely worried about my drinking so I pretended to slow down but every chance I got, when she was either sleeping or running to the store I would make a quick trip to the gas station convenience store next door and got more beer which I hid in various places around the room. She knew I was drinking but I concealed how much; I was repeating the same damn patterns with her as I had with J.

The baby was starting to show and I was ecstatic and also fucking terrified. I began jogging in the area and also hitting the treadmill at the motel gym when the weather got bad; this was to calm my nerves and try to slow-down the drinking. KM began getting visions and communications from Aiwass-Lucifer; sometimes she would go into a trance either after sex or when she was in the shower. KM received a word from him which is now the name of my publishing company: Babiazna. He told her that this was one of His most ancient names; she also kept getting visions of a "purple" place which I immediately recognized as something called "the mauve zone" from one of Grant's books. Since this is not the place to go into esoteric ramblings about magic or mysticism I'll simply state that the "mauve zone" is an astral location in which one can communicate with various preternatural beings. I'll be writing a book about all the details of these communications with Aiwass at a later time, for those that are interested. It will be called For the Love of the Serpent.

KM was exhausted, filled with anxiety and experiencing a lot of weird trances from Aiwass that were literally starting to drive her crazy. She spent a lot of time sleeping, but always a fitful sleep with nightmares and visions; when she wasn't sleeping we were having sex which would make her drop off to sleep and experience more visions. When awake and speaking with me she was always crying and sobbing telling me how much she missed her home, her dog and her bar. She didn't want to leave me but she felt terrible being ripped from her old life; she had spent many years building up a particular lifestyle through dedication and hard work and now it was gone. She was also suffering through post-trauma from the rape that I wasn't aware of and another thing I learned about her; in her teens she had been in a horrible car accident that had broken 75% of the bones in her body! The doctors couldn't believe she had survived but they were pretty certain she would never walk again; she proved them wrong by willing herself to walk. It was a slow process but through an incredible amount of will and unbelievable strength she did it!

Our finances were always a worry but we knew I would soon receive the money from the sale of my home; it would give us a good cushion. But it didn't. When the check came it was a measly seventeen thousand dollars! I know that sounds like a lot, but we were without a home with a baby on the way; this was devastating. KM became more and more distraught, crying all the time now; at one point I couldn't take it anymore. I thought to myself, "I can't take care of this woman and our baby; I haven't held a regular job for years, I've got a severe drinking problem with no end in sight; what the fuck was I going to do?!" So I took the cowards' way out. I had seventeen grand, I could stay in this motel, pay the bill until my cash runs out, continue to drink myself into a stupor and eventually find a nice rope and good secure place to hang myself. Seriously, this was my plan! I had made a mess of my life and there was no other way out. Why take this beautiful woman and our baby down with me? I stupidly thought that she'd be better off with her husband; he had money, she could take back control of her bar, our child could be raised in a good household (again, not being aware of the rape), go to a good College and live securely. So I had to make a hard decision.

I told her to "Get out, go back home. You're always whining about how much you miss your old life, well go back to it!" She began to cry and I turned cold and mean. "No! Get the fuck out! You're better off back there anyway. I've got a little money, I'll figure something out. Get out! I'm tired of your damn crying!" It broke my heart to see her standing there sobbing uncontrollably; it breaks my heart to think about it now. I felt devastated, torn apart but I didn't see any other way; my life was destroyed but at least our child could be raised properly. She gathered all of her things and started carrying them out the door; I didn't help, I just sat there drinking beer after beer. She turned to me one last time as if to say, "Please don't make me do this." "Get out!" I screamed.

She slouched, turned towards the door and shuffled to the car. I kicked the door shut with my boot and collapsed on the floor; I crawled over to one of my hiding places and retrieved another can of beer; I cracked it open and drank the whole thing in just a few seconds. I tossed the empty can across the room and grabbed another. Fuck. I lay on my back on the floor and stared up at the ceiling, eyeing the pipes that ran from wall to wall. Hmmmm....I thought to myself; I wonder if that would hold me? Now I'll just need to find some good strong rope. Fuck.

Handcuffed, Searched & Loaded

In my pathetic state I just kept drinking and stumbling to the gas station for more bad food, beer and wine. I couldn't rouse myself to exercise but I was able to locate some woman I knew for texting and sexting. No amount of sensory indulgence could get rid of this horrible, rotten feeling that kept surging through me. In one last desperate attempt to return to my previous life I even got in touch with J. and begged her to take me back; she wasn't having any of it. Who could blame her? She was finally rid of this nasty egomaniacal drunk. The next step was to make plans for my suicide. Why not? It had been a good life, mostly; I'd toured much of the world, put out some great albums and had a lot of sex adventures; perhaps it was simply time to check-out. A lot of semi-famous and actually famous musicians had killed themselves; intentionally and not-so-intentionally. I may as well keep to the stereotype and join the crowd.

I had forced KM to leave because she was so miserable here with me and missed her old life so I thought I was doing her and the baby a favor; they could be with her husband, have all the comforts of life and the boy could go to a good College. So my options were; bring her back to me and try to straighten up or kill myself now and they could live happily ever after. I can't remember who contacted who first but KM and I began Facebook messaging, texting and calling each other; initially I just wanted to know how she was doing back home and she told me flat-out that she was so miserable without me that it was killing her. She said she barely ever moved from the sofa and every night she slept alone in her own room; she asked how I was doing and I told her that I was miserable, drinking too much and just didn't see a way out of this situation, but at least I knew that she and the baby were ok.

"But I'm not ok" she told me. "I can't do this without you; I miss you and love you so much." "Well..." I mumbled "Maybe you should come back." "What did you say?" she asked. "I said, maybe you should come back. I'm an idiotic drunken mess, I've been thinking about killing myself but maybe it would be best if you came back." "Do you mean it?" she whispered "Do you really mean it?" Fuck. "Yes, I mean it. I need you; I'm dying over here. I need you back." And that was it. The same day she got in her car and started driving back to Louisiana.

I wish I could say that her returning to me made me quit drinking, but it didn't ; but I knew I was going to have to slow my roll and cut back until I could completely quit. That night she pulled into the Mainstay parking lot; I was outside drinking a beer and smoking a cigarette. She dashed out of the car and straight into my arms; we held each other like that for quite some time. "I'm going to quit drinking" I told her "I have to do it gradually but I'm going to quit." "I know you will" she said "I know you can do it; I'm right here with you." After carrying her things into the room we immediately started counting the cash I had left; it wasn't much but it was a few thousand dollars and after looking online we found a carriage house near-by that my money could cover for a few months. When we went to look at it, we loved it; it had two stories, the main bedroom was at the top with a glass door leading to a deck outside, two bathrooms, a guest bedroom a kitchen and on the Land-Ladies' property just over a tiny fence was a baby pig named Stella. The only thing that worried me was that there was an iron-wrought spiral staircase that led up to the bedroom; I thought that would be dangerous for her and the baby so we decided that once she got too big we could sleep downstairs in the guest bedroom.

Now we just needed to get jobs and work on building up a good flow of money. I was terrified at the thought of having to work; I hadn't had a job in many years and didn't know what the fuck I could do. KM said, "Well, you're a writer; you've written a couple of books and a bunch of articles, why don't you write a book on our experiences together; we've been through some crazy shit and it would make a great story." Of course! Why hadn't I thought of that? I could write a semi-fictional account of the last few months, something like Foucault's Pendulum; a mixture of mystery and the occult with some action thrown in and BAM! A best seller! I began fleshing out this story while she started looking for a job. I called the book Demonic Love: Under a Red Moon; I finished it long ago but never followed-through on getting it to a publisher. Maybe someday I'll get it out. This was a good idea but deep-down I knew it wouldn't be a substitute for an actual job, but at least my mortal fear of working would be staved-off for the time being.

I had really slowed down on my drinking; by the time KM had found a job my drinking had completely stopped. Her job however was in Florida! It was temporary but she knew she could make a good amount of cash bartending there until the baby was almost ready to birth. As much as I loved her, her leaving was a fucking relief! I was craving alcohol so badly I could barely contain myself. She left me with a good amount of money; as soon as she drove away I ran right to the liquor store and stocked up on beer; there was a grocery store about a forty-five minute walk from the house. I could buy a lot of nonperishable cheap food some wine, hard booze and a ton of cheap beer. Once I got there though there was no wine or hard booze to be found! None! I got home with the groceries and started wandering the neighborhood, praying I would find a store that carried something stronger than beer! Nope. Nothing; apparently Bossier City Louisiana is not allowed to sell anything stronger then beer! That's alright, I thought; that'll be better for me; just beer. It will be easier to quit once KM got home.

So I drank beer; a lot of beer. A case or more a day; after a while it wasn't even effecting me. Fuck. I wanted to get drunk; I needed to get fall-down stinking fucking drunk. That's when I discovered that the bar-restaurant down the street had every type of wine, beer and hard booze I could imagine. Eureka! I was saved. There was one problem; I knew that the amount of cash that KM had left me wouldn't cover the bar tab so I decided to grab one of the cards we had in the house and hop on down to drink to my hearts' content; my oasis. Trouble was I had grabbed the wrong card; I had grabbed the card that was maxed-out with no money on it whatsoever.

To say that I made a nuisance of myself there would be an understatement; I have a very shady recollection of downing many vodka martinis and hitting on the waitresses. Apparently I was bragging that I was a rock star and had recently been having conversations with the Devil! To make matters worse, when I gave the bartender my card to pay the bill it was, of course, declined. "Oh right" I said "I grabbed the wrong card. I'll walk to my house and come back with the good one; it'll take me five minutes" This was true; the carriage house was literally only a block away. But no; the proprietor was not having any of it; he told me I needed to pay my bill now or he was going to call the police. "C'mon man; I'll leave you this card and my picture ID, hell, I'll leave my whole wallet. Just let me walk down the street and I'll be right back." Maybe if I hadn't been such a drunken asshole hitting on his employees and blathering on about my old band and The Devil he would have let me go. No chance. "Fuck you man!" I yelled, "I'm outta here!" and I stumbled to the front door; he chased me outside and then pulled out a knife which he held to my wrist, not letting me go.

"What the fuck you doing, man? Let the fuck go of me!" He did not let go and in my drunken state I was in no condition to fight him. As I continued to try and pry myself loose the police showed up; I was handcuffed, searched and loaded into the back of the police car. I tried to explain my situation but nobody was listening to me; in my stupor I probably wasn't making much sense. I looked down the street and could almost see the carriage house; so close yet so far away. Damn. I was driven to the local jail, gave up my belongings and escorted to a very uncomfortable cement cell with thick metal bars; this was the drunk-tank. I figured they'd let me sleep it off and release me in the morning but this was not the case. In a couple of hours they booked me, took my mug shot, gave me a ratty orange jumpsuit and pushed me into a huge room with a hundred or so other inmates and a bunch of metal bunk beds. What the fuck is happening, I thought to myself? This can't be real; this must be a detox nightmare or something. It wasn't. I found the bunk with the number they assigned me, lay down to try and sleep and to ignore all the other jail-birds that were squawking around me. "Well Vadge Moore" I thought "You've really done it this time; you've really fucked up."

AnViL Dropped

Over-all the time I spent in jail wasn't that bad; the other inmates were quite nice and polite, nobody got shanked, no fights broke out, the guards didn't have to tear gas the lot of us and I was not raped. The worst part about it was the community bathroom which was only a couple of toilets, behind a waist-high cement wall so that when you sat down to crap you'd have a little privacy. The second worst part about my "incarceration" was the food; I've travelled many parts of the world, I've had spectacular meals in Paris, cooked by our hosts at the club, eaten delicious grandmothers' recipe dishes in Tokyo, Japan, had scrumptious meals in Italy and eaten the foulest, nastiest garbage you can imagine at seedy truck stops across the US not to mention the worst of the worst at soup-kitchens in SF during the eighties; but nothing comes close to how bland, odd, strangely colored and more akin to cardboard than food was this Shreveport Louisiana jail meal! Suffering from a horrible hang over, I couldn't even touch this food let alone put it in my mouth. A guy sitting next to me at the mess table asked if I was going to eat it; I said "Hell no. Have at it, buddy" and slid the tray over to him.

Other than trying to figure out how I was going to hold my shit in so I didn't have to use the crapper I also contemplated how I was going to get out of there; I was a little hazy on what I had done but I guessed I hadn't murdered anyone otherwise they would not have had me in the general population. Lying on my bunk I noticed they had let me keep my shoes while everybody else wore slippers; the orange jumpsuit I was wearing was starting to itch in all the worst places. Just as I was dropping off to sleep I heard, "Madison? Tim Madison? Come with me!" I shook my head clear, stood up and made a bolt for the door. "Right here; I'm coming!" As I passed my mess-table neighbor, he high-fived me and said "Thanks for the grub!"

What was happening, where was I going? Are they letting me go; did the bar owner drop the charges? KM is in Florida so she couldn't have bailed me out; and that's where I was wrong. She'd been texting me since just after I was arrested. Sensing that something was wrong when her texts and calls went unanswered, she panicked. She started calling around to all the local hospitals fearing the worst and when she didn't turn up any results she began checking the jails; bingo! She found me. Being a few hundred miles away she couldn't come get me herself so she located a bail bondsman that could bail me out and pick me up. After I was given back all my belongings and a date for me to appear in court I was escorted out of the building into a parking lot. Bleary-eyed and hungover I looked around to try and locate my whereabouts so I could figure out how to walk back to the carriage house. That's when I heard a car horn honk and a voice yell, "Tim Madison?" Uh, what the fuck? "Yes," I replied. "KM sent me here to get you out. Get in the truck." I hung my head in shame and crawled into the passenger seat. He dropped me off at the house and drove away; I fumbled for my keys praying to god that I had left some beer in the fridge. Sure enough; beer! I was saved! I cracked open two and guzzled both in about a minute. You'd think after my experience of the last twenty four hours that I might have decided to swear off drinking, but not me. After finishing the twelve-pack I went scrounging through the house for some change to get more. KM called me and told me what she had done; I apologized profusely and tried to explain what happened but couldn't remember much.

When it seemed things couldn't get any worse that's when the next shoe dropped; really more like an anvil. KM had not been feeling well and decided to go to the local hospital to get a check-up and see how the baby was doing; that's when she was told there was no second heart beat inside of her; nothing. After doing more tests they concluded that the child, our boy, our

Jonathon Embry Madison had died inside her; still born. They had to dilate her cervix to get him out of her; she delivered our baby dead. He had lived approximately seven months. When she gave me this horrible news over the phone I couldn't speak; she was sobbing uncontrollably but I just went numb. Dead? Couldn't be; our boy was supposed to be a special child brought to us by Aiwass-Lucifer himself. Wow. This was the whole reason we got together in the first place and now he was gone. Now what? At first I surmised that he was probably hurt in the car crash and later died within her from trauma sustained from that accident; or maybe he was hurt or killed during the many instances of her husband physically abusing her. Turns out that it was pre-eclampsia, a dangerous pregnancy complication that can lead to serious and fatal complications for both baby and mother. All we knew was that our baby was dead.

It goes without saying that I spent every penny I could find on beer; no hard booze but a shit-ton of beer. She finished her job in Florida and then returned to the carriage house; when she walked in the front door we held each other and cried standing in the doorway for a very long time. Afterwards we were both very numb; the pain hadn't completely set in for me but I knew it would eventually. I believe we both were thinking privately "Well, if the reason we were brought together is gone why stay together?" We failed. Maybe we should part ways.

Then one day I was coming down the spiral staircase and saw her asleep on the couch below me; my heart stopped. She was so beautiful, she is perfect for me, I love her; I love her so very much. I can't ever leave her. And so it would be. Now we needed a plan; our stay at the carriage house was coming to an end and we needed to find a new home. Since she had such an impressive work record she started applying for bar and restaurant jobs around the country. At this time KM began experiencing more trances and visions; they seemed to increase as soon as we were back together. After piecing through these visions we realized that she was going through the Abyss. This is a major Thelemic initiatory ordeal!

Soon afterwards she accepted a job offer in New Orleans, Louisiana as General Manager of a restaurant just outside of the French Quarter. Prior to this offer I had severely slowed down my drinking and had actually quit, stopped completely! How long this would last I did not know; I had been jogging every day and doing yoga, getting stronger and stronger. When I heard we would be moving to New Orleans, the drinking capital of the world, I paused for one second and said to myself, "I will never have another drink again." That was nine years ago and I have stuck to that pledge, not breaking it once. We packed up our things, put some of it in a storage shed in Shreveport and fit what we could into the tiny car. As we drove away towards our new life I was happy, excited and sober for the first time in years.

When You Call, They Come

Along with the job at the restaurant KM was also given a flat in the French Quarter for us to move into for the first few months; it was right at the corner of Gov. Nichols and Decatur streets in the heart of The Quarter. It was beautiful with hard-wood floors and big windows looking right down onto Decatur Street. I had heard that since Hurricane Katrina crime had climbed pretty rapidly but I was not prepared for what I saw one afternoon; I was sitting on our sofa reading a book when suddenly I heard a hell of a commotion coming from outside. As I peered out of the window I saw bright-red fresh blood puddled up on the sidewalk; I see a bloody knife tossed on the ground and catch a slumped-over figure stumbling across the street, holding his gut. A French Quarter stabbing, right outside our window; welcome to New Orleans! This was not the same New Orleans I had seen during my time with The Dwarves; this Crescent City was meaner, nastier with much more corporate control. The Corporate vultures had swooped in and taken charge of this lovely town after Katrina. It still retains its' old charm but not in the same way I had remembered. Around this time I see a young homeless punk rocker hanging around our neighborhood; he's got a Dwarves patch prominently displayed on his leather jacket and one morning I was awakened by the sounds of the record The Dwarves Are Young & Good Looking blaring out of somebody's car windows; a stabbing on the street and Dwarves fans; very appropriate.

KM's job at the restaurant was challenging to say the least; a once thriving business, it had gone to ruin with cooks high on heroin nodding off on the ovens and rats the size of small dogs terrorizing the place. At one point, early in the job she had to break up a serious knife-fight between two cooks; throughout her time at this job there were numerous instances of employees having to deal with crime and violence at their residences. One evening a cook had witnessed the shooting death of two of his friends. As for the rats, KM had access to the security cameras through her phone; one night at our apartment she called me over and said, "Look at this. This fucking King Rat knows that we keep a lot of food in this metal safe; he comes after hours and just stares at the safe, trying to figure out a way to get in it!" She hands me her phone and I see a rat the size of a very large raccoon staring fixedly at the safe. This rat was fucking big!

As for me, I hadn't had a regular job since 2004 when I was a ground-man on the tree crew. I'd been working on the semi-fictional account of our story Demonic Love, but it was nowhere near finished; the chance of me making a living off of my writing was pretty slim. One day we're walking down Royal Street in the French Quarter enjoying the atmosphere when we pass an occult bookstore called Starling Magical. KM looks at me and says, "Why don't you go in there and apply for a job?" An occult bookstore job; that would be perfect! I walk in and begin talking to the owners Claudia and Jan (pronounced Yan); Claudia asks me if I can do any readings. Still stuck In my ego-centrist mindset I think that she's recognized me and wants me to do some book readings! "Of course" I say "I've got a book that was published five years ago and some new unpublished stuff that I'd love to read here!" Claudia looks at me quizzically and replies, "No. Tarot readings; can you do Tarot readings?" Oh, duh. I had been using Crowley's Thoth Tarot for a number of years to give me pointers and suggestions for what life-path to follow and I'd used the Thoth deck to decipher messages KM had been getting from Aiwass; so, sure! "I can definitely do Tarot readings."

On top of helping clean up the store and arranging the library in the room directly past the shop-proper, I also began giving Tarot reading to customers in another side-room. The readings were quite successful and I made some good money and tips. A lot of my time was spent sitting in the shop and shooting the shit with Jan and Claudia, two fascinating individuals. A couple of the high-lights of me working there was watching the Mardi-Gras parade pass by the store and seeing Tom Cruise film some scenes for one of his movies directly across the street.

At the French Quarter flat KM began receiving messages from Aiwass after going into a trance; at first she tried communicating these messages by voice, but it would manifest in a very gravelly growl that made me think of Linda Blair in The Exorcist movie; appropriate I suppose, but later I would see film footage on You Tube of a Tibetan Buddhist ceremony; Buddhist oracles receiving messages from deities. The person chosen as an oracle would go into a trance and have a similar sounding voice; I wanted to mention this before the reader got a cheesy impression of us summoning the Devil and his voice manifesting in some gross Hollywood Satanic-possession caricature. Regardless the voice communication was very difficult to understand so I would hand KM a pen and a notebook and she would write down what words she was receiving. Again, I know some people will find the authenticity of this experience hard to believe, but I'm just describing what I saw and heard. I had spent many years studying Magick and practicing magical ceremonies and it now seemed that, through performing the Star Ruby and Liber Reguli rituals I had actually summoned something! I recall the words written by Crowley in his final book Magick Without Tears, "When you call, They come." Holy shit, he wasn't kidding!

At this time I began practicing a daily meditation routine that continues into the present day; meditation and exercise (specifically jogging) are the two things that have really helped me in changing my patterns of thinking and behaving. Everything that I had learned at my three trips to New Perceptions rehab also had been a very significant asset to say the least! Stanley, Thelma, Gregory and the rest of the crew there had figuratively speaking beaten into my brain all the methods I would need to stay sober. It's frequently said that you can't get sober until you've hit rock bottom; the night spent in Bossier City trying to figure out if the pipes on the ceiling would hold my dangling body, my short stint in Shreveport jail in that itchy orange jumpsuit and KM and I losing our baby was definitely rock bottom. It was only upwards from there or it would have been my death.

HEaLtH & HappinEss

Our free-time at the French Quarter apartment was up so we were going to have to find another apartment to rent. KM found a cute little place on Esplanade Street a block from City Park in New Orleans; it was in a large seven-story building called, appropriately, The Esplanade. My job at Starling, which was only part time, wasn't going to bring in enough money for rent and bills so I found a job as dishwasher at an Italian restaurant just two to three blocks from our apartment. KM made me feel better about this menial job by telling me that legendary musician Alex Chilton from the Box Tops also spent years in New Orleans as a dishwasher; she knew him at the time and told me he seemed very content. This was good enough for me.

Our apartment on the seventh floor was small but comfortable; through our windows we could look down and see an above-ground cemetery that is part and parcel of the entire New Orleans area giving our stay there a very spooky but cool vibe. We performed a lot of menstrual sex magic with messages coming from Aiwass at an incredible pace; as mentioned these communications will be the subject of a book I'll be writing called For the Love of The Serpent; there I will go into much more detail about these experiences. I finished and had published a book of my prose writings called Malevolence; a combination of the prose from Chthonic Prose & Theory and newer material I had been working on in Atlanta and Denver.

I felt I could take a breath and look back over the last year with a fresh and sober mind; I thought of our escape from our unhappy marriages, our deep love for one another...and then I thought of Jonathon, our child who we lost. That's when I broke down in tears; I receiving messages from Aiwass the entire time.

It was around this period that my interests turned toward Buddhism; especially Tibetan Tantric Buddhist Chogyam Trungpa; I read every single one of his books I could find from online downloads. I realize now that my morning meditation routine was changing me at a very fundamental level; it was making me a nicer person. I understood that I needed to be better for KM; I'd had a terrible temper my entire life; anger had influenced and driven me for as long as I could remember; it certainly contributed to my drinking problem and helped create so many of the situations that led me to drink. Buddhism and many of its' practices allows me to put the brakes on that anger; if it makes me a better partner for KM and a better person in general then I could see nothing wrong with engaging in Buddhism full time. This is what I've done. As time passed I went directly to the Buddhist Sutras to find the beginnings of Buddhism particularly through the work of Bhikkhu Bodhi. I know I will always be a Thelemite at heart; it was Crowley's initiatory system that introduced me to the love of my life, helped me get sober and made me a healthier, more disciplined person then I have ever been before. I guess you could pigeonhole me as a "Thelemic-Buddhist" at this point in my life; but I know that the spiritual journey I'm on will never come to an end, not in this lifetime or any other.

Through a job recruiter KM found a General Manager position in North Texas; she also found a house online in the same town: three bedrooms, two baths and a huge backyard for our dog. I took a position as a convenience store clerk nearby; the job is enjoyable but it's not without its dangers; one evening I was sprayed in the eyes with mace and robbed for a handful of scratch-off tickets. No harm done, but I never want to be sprayed with mace again!

So there you have it: twenty-three years of alcohol abuse, sexual perversion, marriage, divorce, rehab, rehab again, rehab one more time, communications with "The Devil", sobriety and finally happiness. I have no fucking idea how I made it out alive with very few physical or psychological scars; I'm happier and healthier then I have ever been and I feel that I can enter the twilight of my life with a great deal of satisfaction. This has been a life well-lived.

But that's not all; in the final book of this trilogy I will explore my life from birth, through adolescence into the tumultuous teens, culminating in my twenties and joining The Dwarves. Stay tuned, dear reader; that book will also be one wild fucking ride.

Vadge Moore (Tim Madison) was born in 1967 in the San Francisco Bay Area. At an early age he developed a love of two things; writing and rock music. As a teenager he became involved with the California Hardcore Punk Scene and was the drummer for Crypt and the Test Subjects. Inspired by Hunter S. Thompson and Black Flag singer Henry Rollins, Vadge began writing, Xeroxing and distributing his own books of prose and poetry. In 1988 he joined a punk band recently relocated from Chicago called The Dwarves, recording and touring with them for a dozen years. Vadge formed his own experimental-noise band called Chthonic Force, releasing two full-length albums and one "best of" compilation. In the year 2000 Vadge left The Dwarves. In 2005 he moved to Atlanta, Georgia where he wrote the books Chthonic Prose & Theory and Malevolence. Vadge has written articles for numerous occult publications on the subject of Magician/Occultist Aleister Crowley. Vadge now resides in the American South with the love of his life and their dog. My Life After The Dwarves is the second book of a trilogy that will explore the life and times of this fascinating individual.

www.ingramcontent.com/pod-product-compliance
Lightning Source LLC
Chambersburg PA
CBHW031901090426
42741CB00005B/591